Hitler's Theology

Continuum Resources in Religion and Political Culture
Series Editors: Graham Ward and Michael Hoelzl, The University of
Manchester, UK

Aimed at undergraduates studying in this area, titles in this series look
specifically at the key topics involved in the relationship between religion
and politics, taking into account a broad range of religious perspectives,
and presenting clear, approachable texts for students grappling with
often complex concepts.

The New Visibility of Religion, edited by Graham Ward and Michael Hoelzl

Remoralizing Britain, edited by Peter Manly Scott, Christopher R. Baker
and Elaine L. Graham

Postsecular Cities, edited by Justin Beaumont and Christopher Baker

From Political Theory to Political Theology, edited by Péter Losonczi and
Aakash Singh

Hitler's Theology
A Study in Political Religion

Rainer Bucher

Translated by
Rebecca Pohl

Edited and with an Introduction by
Michael Hoelzl

continuum

Continuum International Publishing Group

The Tower Building 80	Maiden Lane
11 York Road	Suite 704
London SE1 7NX	New York NY 10038

www.continuumbooks.com

Original published in German as *Hitlers Theologie* © Echter Verlag GmbH

This English language edition © Continuum, 2011

British Library Cataloguing-in-Publication Data
A catalogue record for this book is available from the British Library.

ISBN: HB: 978-1-4411-9679-8
       PB: 978-1-4411-4179-8

Library of Congress Cataloguing-in-Publication Data
Bucher, Rainer, 1956-
   [Hitlers Theologie. English]
   Hitler's theology : a study in political religion / Rainer Boucher;
   translated by Rebecca Pohl ; with an introduction by Michael Hoelzl.
   p. cm.
   Includes bibliographical references (p.) and index.
   ISBN 978-1-4411-9679-8–ISBN 978-1-4411-4179-8
   1. Hitler, Adolf, 1889-1945–Religion. 2. Hitler, Adolf, 1889-1945–Political
   and social views. I. Pohl, Rebecca. II. Title.

DD247.H5B723313 2011
943.086092--dc22

                                                    2011002791

Typeset by Newgen Imaging Systems Pvt Ltd, Chennai, India
Printed and bound in Great Britain

Contents

Mottos

Thus I believe to be acting according to the wishes of the almighty Creator: By fighting off the Jew, I am fighting for the work of the Lord.

Adolf Hitler, Mein Kampf, 1925

At the heart of our program you will not find any mysterious presentiments, rather you will find succinct realization and hence open avowal. Since we place the sustenance and securing of a creature created by God at the center of this realization and avowal, we sustain God's creation, and it is in this manner that we serve this will. We do not do so at a new cult site bathed in mysterious twilight, but rather, in the open, for the Lord to see.

Adolf Hitler, Party Congress Speech, 1938

The fellow is a catastrophe. But that is no reason why we should not find him interesting, as a character and as an event. Consider the circumstances. Here is a man possessed of a bottomless resentment and a festering desire for revenge; a man ten times a failure, extremely lazy, incapable of steady work; a man who has spent long periods in institutions; a disappointed bohemian artist; a total good-for-nothing. And here is a people obsessed with powerful though far less justifiable feelings of defeat and inferiority, and unable to think of anything save how to retrieve its lost 'honor.' And then he – who had learned nothing, and in his dreamy, obstinate arrogance never would learn anything; who had neither technical nor physical discipline, could not sit a horse, or drive a car, or fly a plane, or do aught that men do, even to begetting a child – he develops the one thing needful to establish a connection between him and the people: a gift of oratory. It is oratory unspeakably inferior in kind, but magnetic in its effect on the masses: a weapon of definitely histrionic, even hysterical power, which he thrusts into the nation's wound and turns round. He rouses the populace with images of his own insulted grandeur, deafens it with promises, makes out of the people's sufferings a vehicle for his own greatness, his ascent to fantastic heights, to unlimited power, to incredible compensations and over-compensations. He rises to such a pitch of glorification and awe-inspiring sanctity that anyone who in the past had wronged him – when he was unknown, despised and rejected, becomes straightway a child of the evil one and merits the most shameful and frightful death.

Thomas Mann, 'That Man Is My Brother', 1938

Every word that issues from Hitler's mouth is a lie. When he says peace he means war and when he most sinfully names the name of the Almighty, he means the force of evil, the fallen angel, Satan. His mouth is the stinking throat of hell and his power is fundamentally depraved.

Fourth Pamphlet of the White Rose, 1942

Translator's Note

For this translation I have chosen a literal approach both to the text of the study itself as well as to the texts it in turn quotes. Given the methodology of the study – the analysis of historical primary sources – this has posed a number of distinct challenges that also spill over into quotations from secondary material. In order to resolve these challenges, I have chosen the following procedures:

Where available, I have used existing English translations both of primary source material (e.g. Hitler's speeches, Speer's memoirs) and of secondary material (e.g. Joachim Fest). Where no English translation was readily available, I have translated the material (both primary and secondary) myself. In cases where the author has used a German translation of an English source, I have here quoted from the English original (e.g. Ian Kershaw). The references in the footnotes and the information in the bibliography correspond to the details of the actually quoted texts in the present translation.

There is one exception to this: the author makes extensive use both of Henry Picker's *Hitlers Tischgespräche im Führerhauptquartier 1941–1942* and *Monologe im Führerhauptquartier 1941–1944. Die Aufzeichnungen Heinrich Heims*, edited by W. Jochmann. There is an English translation of these two texts entitled *Hitler's Table Talk 1941–1944*. It was translated by Norman Cameron and R. H. Stevens, with an introduction by H.R. Trevor-Roper and was published in 1953 (by Weidenfeld and Nicolson, London). The publication history of these documents is extremely fraught, however, even before questions of translation are considered. Copyright issues have resulted in the two different German versions and the translation is purportedly based on a third set of documents. As the English translation is not only of dubious origin but also of dubious intent and ideological underpinning, I have chosen to translate the German source material myself. (For a discussion of this problematic see: Richard C. Carrier, ' "Hitler's Table Talk": Troubling Finds'. *German Studies Review*, Vol. 26, No. 3, (Oct 2003): 561–76.)

Various translations of *Mein Kampf* are available. I have chosen to use James Murphy's 1939 version for a number of reasons. It was the first full-length translation published in Britain and it was de facto authorized by the German authorities (ex-negativo: no legal action was taken against the publisher, Hurst & Blackett). It has also been classified as sympathetic to the cause (cf. Stefan

Baumgarten, *Translating Hitler's* Mein Kampf: *A corpus-aided discourse-analytical study* (2009)) which perhaps allows it to more readily express Hitler's emotive and ideological pronouncements. While translation is always a fraught process, and perhaps none more so than this particular case, a decision had to be made. The situatedness of the translation should hence be borne in mind when reading the text. There are singular instances where I have commented on the translation in footnotes.

Specialist Nazi terminology for which there is no satisfactory English equivalent has been left untranslated and is rendered in italics and explained in a separate glossary (p. 124). The explanations of these terms are based on the following resource: Robert Michael and Karin Doerr, *Nazi-Deutsch/Nazi German: An English Lexicon of the Language of the Third Reich* (London: Greenwood, 2002). Occasionally I have inserted German terms in square brackets into already translated sources in order to provide a fuller idea of the referent.

A note on *völkisch*: I have chosen not to translate this particular term and so it appears in its German rendition. However, I have adapted the grammatical forms in correspondence with English rather than German grammar. Other sources quoted in the study offer translations of the term and in these instances, I have maintained their suggestions (Max Domarus' English version suggests 'volkic' (cf. Chapter 3) and James Murphy suggests 'folk-idea' (cf. Chapter 5)).

My gratitude goes to Dr Michael Hoelzl for his advice on questions of theology and to Irene Huhulea and Anne Stähr for their attention to detail, both English and German. And to Iain Bailey for his support in matters not only of language.

Preface

Hitler's theology is intellectually crude, its racism is abominable and its God is a numinous monster. It harbours no mercy, no charity and thus also no peace.[1] But it became – and truly all theology aims to be this – practical. This is not the only, but it is the irrefutable, reason to study it.

For the 'break with civilization' [*Zivilisationsbruch*][2] signified by Hitler's National Socialist project affected everyone and everything, occurred from the centre of German society and with strong and longstanding support from its elites, as well as broad parts of the population.[3] Hitler's God possessed a great power. It took the united armies of the Soviet Union, America, Great Britain and many others to break it. Incidentally, nobody could guarantee this: Hitler's God could also have triumphed through him.

It is unnecessary to disprove Hitler's theology: it did that itself. But it is necessary to study it. After all, as Ian Kershaw rightly asserts: 'Hitler's mark on the century has been deeper than that of' any other political leader.[4] Regardless of all justified questions of how this physically inconspicuous, petty-bourgeois foreigner, laden with complexes, formally uneducated and lacking in any real work experience or organizational talent succeeded in becoming the most powerful man of the German Reich, and temporarily of Europe, what social and cultural structures and sentiments sustained his ascent, how he anticipated, utilized and steered these, the fact remains: National Socialism was Hitler's project; he enforced it, and nobody even came close to Hitler's singular position of power.[5] After all, the entire country – with the exception of the brave men and women of the few resistance groups – followed him toward disaster.

This book is written by a Catholic theologian. I have studied Hitler academically because I wanted to know why he fascinated some 'progressive' theologians of the 1930s. What induced innovative theologians, who were sensitive to the present and later rightfully gained renown, to enthusiastically welcome Hitler? What problems weighed on them that made them see a fascinating solution in Hitler's social project of all things? What religious structures and what theological discourses, I asked, did this social project offer that made it so attractive to them?

I did not want to content myself with the allusion, which is indisputably correct, to the political naïveté even of great theologians. For in opting for

Hitler these theologians were evidently concerned with the 'vitality' of their Catholic Church and its ability to engage with and remain relevant in the present; with the question of how Church can continue to exist in the condition of modernity that has become vexingly plural. This did not seem self-evident to them and Hitler's project, of all things, seemed to make it possible again.

The dynamic of modernization and the intense access to personal engagement fascinated not only his own followers. For it was exactly this, dynamism and the intensity of personnel, that the Church lacked – at least precisely in the eyes of some of the more innovative theologians. In any case, Hitler's offer was more attractive for his contemporaries than it might seem in hindsight and with the knowledge of his monstrous crimes. Hitler appeared to enable modernization without pluralization, and thus without the relativization of his own claims to validity, as well as without the liberal emancipation of the subject.

I owe my personal interest to the Catholic Youth Association of my home-town of Bayreuth. In 1973 the Catholic Youth Association managed to organize a trip to Poland, still part of the Communist regime at that time, which I was happy to join. We visited Breslau, Krakow, Częstochowa – and also the Auschwitz concentration camp memorial. I realized there that the ground of civilization is thin under our feet and that it is threatened from the centre and not from the margins of society, and I have not forgotten it since.

This book is based on research that I undertook a while ago and presented to the research community in the context of my Habilitation in pastoral theology, *Kirchenbildung in der Moderne. Konstitutionsprinzipien der deutschen katholischen Kirche.*[6] The results have been updated and are herewith presented to a broader audience with an interest in history.

I thank Ottmar Fuchs, Maximilian Liebmann, Lucia Scherzberg, Norbert Reck, Katharina von Kellenbach and Claus-Eckehard Bärsch for stimulating exchanges of ideas across disciplinary borders.

I am grateful to Michael Hoelzl for taking the initiative to translate this book into English, to supervize the translation which has been carefully carried out by Rebecca Pohl. I also want to express my sincere gratitude to Continuum and to Kirsty Shaper in particular, for their assistance and extraordinary support to make this project happen. I also want to take this opportunity to mention that Michael Hoelzl's preface lucidly illuminates from the religio-political standpoint what I intended to achieve with the present theological study.

I dedicate this book to Ernst Ludwig Grasmück on his 75th birthday in grateful memory of my years studying Church history with him.

Rainer Bucher
Graz, January 2011

Notes

[1] However, this does not mean that it is a 'religion of war' [*Kriegsreligion*], as Schirrmacher argues in *Hitlers Kriegsreligion*. The war is certainly the inevitable consequence of the implementation of this theology, but it is not its aim: its aim is the 'idyll' of the Aryan/German *Volksgemeinschaft*. Schirrmacher's study, which was published shortly after the manuscript for the present book was finalized, deserves an extensive critical appraisal.

[2] Cf.: Diner, *Zivilisationsbruch*. 'Break with civilization' here signifies the devastation of all confidence in the ability of civilization to exercise even minimal control over the State's actions and the fact, for instance, 'that the unfounded extermination of humans has become possible and actual.' (31)

[3] Cf.: Falter, *Hitlers Wähler;* Kershaw, *Hitler I,* xxixf.

[4] Kershaw, *Hitler I,* xix.

[5] This does not mean that the major ideas of Hitler's 'Weltanschauung' were in any way original, let alone devised by Hitler himself. But he assembled them in this combination and above all: it was he who empowered them.

[6] Bucher, *Kirchenbildung.*

Introduction: The Study of the Phenomenon of Adolf Hitler in Theology

Michael Hoelzl

Enduring fascination with Adolf Hitler

The most shocking scene in Bernd Eichinger's film *The Downfall*, based on the reconstruction of the last days of the *Third Reich* in the *Führerbunker* by Joachim Fest[1], is Magda Goebbels' proof of unconditional loyalty to Adolf Hitler, the *Führer*. Magda Goebbels is writing a farewell letter to her first born son Harald Quandt, who was at that time a prisoner of war, to explain her decision to take her six children with her:

'My beloved son! We are already in the *Führerbunker* since six days, Dad, your six siblings and I, to end our National Socialist life in a dignified and final way.[. . .] You should know that I have decided to stay against the will of your father and that even last Sunday the *Führer* wanted to help me to escape.[. . .] Our great idea comes to an end and with it all of the beautiful and admirable I have ever known in my life. *The world which will come after the Führer and National Socialism is no longer worth living in and therefore I decided to take the children with me, because they are too valuable for the life after us*; and a merciful God will understand my decision to give them personally their redemption. [. . .] Remain loyal! Loyal to yourself, to people and loyal to your country [. . .].'[2]

On 1 May 1945, a day after Hitler's suicide, Magda Goebbels anesthetized her six infant children and poisoned them with hydrocyanic acid. How can we understand such an incomprehensible deed? How is it possible that Magda Goebbels declined all proposals, refuses all pleas, even from the *Führer*, to save her children. A life, as she is convinced, after the *Führer* was not worth living. Magda Goebbels' decision shows all essential characteristics of religious fanaticism.

First, her decision is an existential one. It is a decision on life or death. Secondly, the option for death is based on unconditional loyalty based on the belief not in 'the' *Führer, but in 'Mein' Führer*. Any other decision appears to be a betrayal of the ultimate goal and therefore, in a negative way, by her action the supreme good is confirmed. Thirdly, the decision is absolute in the sense that everything, not just individual lives, depends on it. Fourthly, the situation is condensed to its uttermost intensity. It is a unique singularity in a person's life and cannot be repeated, like a religious conversion. Finally, the step taken reveals the belief in a transcendent reality. The world as it is cannot be everything. There is a hope for a better future in 'another' reality of whatever kind.

How was this 'quasi- religious fanaticism' possible to emerge? In other words, how can we explain the fascination with Adolf Hitler that mobilized so many people who were prepared to follow at any costs? It seems that Max Weber's analytical category of the 'charismatic leader' is not going far enough to explain the fascination with Adolf Hitler or to understand the phenomenon of Hitler. Weber's famous definition of charismatic leadership is based on the Pauline concept of charisma as a gift from God vested in a single person: '"Charisma" should be called an extraordinary quality of a personality on the basis of which this person is seen to be endowed with supernatural or superhuman, or, at least with specifically extraordinary powers or qualities that are not accessible to everyone; or this person is seen as sent from God or being exemplary and therefore is accepted as "leader" [*Führer*].'[3] Undoubtedly, Hitler was seen as a charismatic person[4] and Joseph Goebbels' diary[5] clearly reveals his unwavering belief in the *Führer's* extraordinary powers and abilities until the end. Nevertheless, the concept of the charismatic leader does not explain why the fascination with Hitler, the belief of so many in his extraordinary qualities, endured even when the downfall was obvious. According to Weber, the authority of the leader is likely to disappear with the leader's failure. 'If the success remains absent permanently, if the charismatically gifted is abandoned by his God or loses his magical and heroic powers, moreover; *if his leadership does not create welfare for the governed*, then his charismatic authority is likely to disappear.'[6] This was clearly not the case with Adolf Hitler. The concept of the charismatic leader is also inappropriate in an analytical sense, in attempting toexplain the fact that there is still a fascination with the phenomenon Hitler today and as an ideal-typical concept it is not precise enough to examine the people's concrete demands that National Socialism and its leader promised to satisfy. Maybe, that is the reason why Rainer Bucher in this present study does not refer to it.

Temptations as unfounded promises

Hitler's Theology is written by a practical theologian. It is one of the few detailed studies on the phenomenon of Hitler from an explicit theological standpoint. Rainer Bucher pursues three directions of investigation. First, there is Hitler's use of theological ideas and his own theo-political theory. Second, Bucher raises the question of what he offered the National Socialist movement that appealed to Catholic theologians so that they attempted to reconcile the National Socialist propaganda with their own desire for a renewal of the Church. Thirdly, how could 'Hitler' be understood in terms of an alternative to the critique of modernity, *Kulturpessimismus* and secularization in general?

All three dimensions of the argument presented here culminate in the question of the fascination with Hitler. In the final tenth chapter of the book, sec. 2: Bucher writes: 'Temptations are unfounded promises, promises that can be made, but can never be kept. Temptations play with yearnings and draw their political strength and their personal fascination from these. The monstrous crimes of National Socialism cover over those elements within it that can develop a lasting attraction. But they play with yearnings and hopes that did not simply disappear with National Socialism.'[7]

Rather than Weber's question of what makes a charismatic leader believable, Bucher asks: what are the false promises that deceived the people and how can we understand why these promises were and remain so convincing?

The first line of investigation provides a theological reading of Hitler's recourse to theological concepts in his speeches. This is done, as mentioned above, from a practical theological perspective, simply because Hitler's 'theology', even though it was not orthodox, in any dogmatic or academic sense of the word, became practical. And practical in this context means politically decisive. To a certain extent Hitler's theology can be called 'political theology'. In his treatise on political theology Carl Schmitt states his famous thesis: 'All significant concepts of the modern theory of the state are secularized theological concepts.'[8] Political theology, therefore, implies a theory of secularization that links theological ideas with political concepts. In a similar way, Bucher quoting Kenneth Burke, points out: 'the patterns of Hitler's thought are a bastardized or caricatured version of religious thought' and 'Hitler appeals by relying upon a bastardization of fundamentally religious patterns of thought.'[9] Hitler's political project gains power by drawing on religious ideas and reinterpreting them in his own theological way. Central to Hitler's project are the idea of community (*völkische Gemeinschaft*) and providence (*Vorsehung*) as legitimation of his role as the chosen leader. Given these two key aspects of Christian theology, it would be more accurate to rephrase Schmitt's thesis with respect to Hitler's theology: All significant concepts of Hitler's modern theory of the 'state' are secularized and bastardized ecclesiological concepts.[10] This is particularly true if we take Hitler's theology of history into account, since no ecclesiology can exist with a theory and theological interpretation of history. This might explain why, for Magda Goebbels, Hitler's death is at the same time the end of National Socialism as an historical epoch. The downfall of the Reich shows truly its apocalyptic dimensions.

The second line of Bucher's investigation[11] concentrates on some well-regarded Catholic theologians' (like Karl Adam, Joseph Lortz and Michael Schmaus) fascination with Hitler. Bucher summarizes this second line of investigation as follows: 'This book is written by a Catholic theologian. I have studied Hitler academically because I wanted to know why he fascinated some "progressive" theologians of the 1930s. What induced innovative theologians, who were sensitive to the present and later rightfully gained renown, to enthusiastically welcome Hitler? What problems weighed on them that made them see a fascinating solution in Hitler's social project of all things? What religious structures and what theological discourses, I asked, did this social project offer that made it so attractive to them?'[12] Some Catholic theologians went further than a policy of appeasement and attempted to elaborate a theology that is capable of reconciling Catholicism with Nazism. Bucher limits his analysis to the Catholic Church and Catholic theologians. In this respect research into the fascination with Hitler's programme from a Protestant, Anglican and even Non-Conformist theological standpoint is still needed – despite some excellent works published recently.[13] Such research from a theological perspective and not merely from a historical one would be even more promising given the different ecclesiologies these denominations have generated and how they responded differently to Hitler's appeal. In other words, it would be interesting to analyze comparatively the responses to Hitler's project, his promises and temptations with respect to different teachings of the nature and purpose of the church as God's people in this world as well as a spiritual community.

The third line of investigation into Hitler's theology reiterates the problem of how the fascination with Hitler can be explained or at least understood. Bucher offers a systematic attempt for explanation rather than an explanation on an individual basis. The central thesis Bucher advocates is that Hitler promised the benefits of modernity (technological progress, social equality, economic growth, betterment of social welfare and foremost unity) without the threats of modernity's demand for pluralism and social disintegration. The fascination with Hitler, as Bucher suggests, cannot be understood without recognizing his paradoxical promise to the people. He appears to the critics of modernity as a modernizer without accepting the shortcomings and discontents of modernity; he promises progress without loss and he gives back a vision or calling to a humiliated people. This was only possible, as Eric Hobsbawm has demonstrated convincingly, because the political tradition of Liberalism and the political trust in parliamentarism had already been eroded before Hitler's rise to power.[14] Hobsbawm illustrates the paradoxical appeal to fascism: 'The novelty of fascism was that, once in power, it refused to play the old political games, and took over completely where it could [. . .] Fascist movements had the elements of revolutionary movements, inasmuch as they contained people who wanted a fundamental transformation of society, often with a notably anti-capitalist and anti-oligarchic edge. However, the horse of revolutionary fascism failed either to start or to run. Hitler rapidly eliminated those who took the "socialist" component in the name of National Socialist Worker's Party seriously – as certainly he did not. The utopia of a return to some kind of little man's Middle Ages, full of hereditary peasant-proprietors, artisan craftsmen like Hans Sachs and girls in blonde plaits, was not a programme that could be realized in major twentieth-century states (except in the nightmare vision of Himmler's plans for a racially purified people), least of all regimes, which like Italian and German Fascism, committed in their way to modernisation and technological advance.'[15]

To a certain extent Bucher and Hobsbawm converge in their explanations of Hitler's success. The main difference, though, is that Hobsbawm argues from a Marxist and therefore economic angle whereas Bucher, a Professor of Practical Theology, argues primarily from a theological perspective.

Research context: Studies in religion and political culture

To concede that Hitler developed his own *theology*, a theology which was very successful in terms of determining people's beliefs and guiding their actions, raises some serious issues. Is it appropriate to talk about Hitler's theology or would be more accurate to talk about Nazi ideology as such? I think Bucher is absolutely right to call it theology rather than to use the more neutral term ideology or *Weltanschauung* because to talk about Hitler's ideology would miss out the crucial point that the fascination with Hitler is based to a great extent on the symbolic power of theological language and the theological reference to a higher, greater transcendent reality. This does not mean that Bucher's analysis of Hitler's theology can be reduced to a simple demonstration of how theological concepts have been (ab)used and reinterpreted by Hitler in order to appeal to the symbolical power of theological ideas. Such a discourse analysis is undertaken in the first line of Bucher's investigation mentioned above. To restrict the investigation simply to a discourse analysis, that is, an analysis of Hitler's rhetoric, would not go far enough in illuminating the phenomenon Adolf Hitler and his mesmerising powers; although, to concentrate on Hitler's speeches and writings is a necessary limitation of the sources for the present analysis. It is true that theologies, ideologies and *Weltanschauungen* have something in common. They are not so much about what we *believe* but what we *do*. Insofar it is only consequent that Hitler's theology is analyzed by a *practical* theologian, that is, from a perspective of theology that understand itself as practically relevant. The distinction between good and bad theology always implies a normative common ground on which this distinction is based on. Therefore Bucher quite explicitly points out: 'Hitler's theology is intellectually crude, its racism is abominable and its God is a numinous monster. It harbours no mercy and no charity and thus also no peace. But it became – and truly all theology aims to be this – practical.'[16]

The fact that the present study is written by a *German* Catholic practical theologian makes the study even more delicate. There is no doubt that research into National Socialism in all its facets is quite different depending on whether it is undertaken within an Anglo-American or German context. In Germany an unbiased academic discussion of Nazism and talk about the fascination with

Hitler was almost impossible until recently. Undertaking, or even suggesting, such a research project without a clear and explicit condemnation of the years 1933–1945 would have been interpreted as a commitment to right wing conservatism or, even worse, as an academic form of crypto-fascism.[17] Since 1945 any academic debate in Germany on Nazism has been already normatively predetermined. In an interesting article, Norbert Reck[18] distinguishes three generations and phases of how German theologians responded to Nazism. The first generation, including Karl Rahner, Heinrich Fries, Michael Schmaus and Romano Guardini, was primarily concerned with the problem of guilt. Their concern was not, as one might think, a direct reflection on National Socialism, they rather called for a return to Christ and they see the roots of Nazism's evil as part of the process of secularization.[19] The second generation, represented by Joseph Ratzinger, Elisabeth Gössmann, Georg Denzler and Johann Baptist Metz, were called the generation of the *Hitlerjugend.* Characteristic for this generation of Catholic theologians is that they were too old not to participate in some sense and too young to be guilty of the deeds of the Nazi regime.[20] They neither belonged to the generation of culprits nor to the generation who questioned their parents about their response to Hitler and asked about their role. The third generation, to which Rainer Bucher belongs, in Reck's classification[21], is characterized by anecdotal rather than personal memory of the Nazi period. For them, and the present study illustrates this approach, the question of how and why Hitler was possible and fascinated so many people is central. In his *Personal Epilogue,*[22] when Bucher talks about his upbringing in Bayreuth, the search for the truth about an increasingly distant history becomes manifest. Following Reck's classification one could argue that since the reunification of Germany a new generation in academia is to come whose understanding of what it is to be German is not so much linked to the question of guilt, collective guilt or hereditary guilt. This generation rather defines its role within a European academic context. The most obvious difference between the Anglo-American and the German discourse on National Socialism is that the former is not marked by these questions of guilt.

Over the last decade the research into religion and politics in its broadest sense has grown exponentially. Despite the vast amount of publications on this topic two strands can be identified. On the one hand there are authors how prefer the term political theology and on the other, there those who prefer the term political religions. The majority of the former pursue a more or less theological goal whereas the latter, following Eric Voegelin, concentrate on the religious elements of totalitarian or fascist politics.[23] With the publication of the quarterly Journal *Totalitarian Movements and Political Religions,* founded in 2000, this area of research has been established on an international level. I think it is fair to say that Bucher's *Hitler's Theology* represents a combination these two strands of research. This is just one reason why his book is insightful for both theologians and non-theologians. It was always the aim and scope of the editors of the series in which *Hitler's Theology* now appears to promote such a crossover and to blur the lines between 'secular' and 'theological' studies. In terms of the author's own academic discipline, that is, Practical Theology, the present study opens new ways of conducting research in this discipline, because it goes beyond the discipline's restriction to pastoral concerns and ecclesial problems.

Notes

[1] Fest, Joachim. *Der Untergang: Hitler und das Ende des Dritten Reiches. Eine historische Skizze* (Berlin: Alexander Fest Verlag, 2002).

[2] See: Longerich, Peter. *Goebbels* (München: Siedler, 2010) pp. 10–11. All translations are mine, except those quotation taken from the present book [translated by Rebecca Pohl], or, except stated otherwise [italics MH].

[3] Weber, Max. *Wirtschaft und Gesellschaft* (Tübingen: Mohr Siebeck, 2002) p. 140.

[4] See for example: Herbst, Ludolf. *Hitler's Messias. Die Erfindung des Deutschen Charismas* (Frankfurt: Fischer Verlag, 2010).

[5] Reuth, Ralf Georg [ed.] *Joseph Goebbels. Tagebücher in fünf Bänden 1924–1945* (München: Piper). See for example the entry of 8 April: 'The *Führer* has to spend incomparable strength of his nerves to maintain his morale in this overcritical situation. But I am still hopeful that he will master the situation. He has always demonstrated his ability to wait for the right moment with sovereign calmness'. Vol. 5, p. 2186.

[6] Weber, Max. *Wirtschaft und Gesellschaft* (Tübingen: Mohr Siebeck, 2002) p. 140.

[7] In this book p. 122

[8] Schmitt, Carl. *Politische Theologie. Vier Kapitel zur Lehre von der Souveränität* (Berlin: Duncker&Humblot, 1996) p. 42.

[9] See p. 13

[10] I owe this thesis to the numerous discussion I had with Professor Graham Ward during our joint translation of Carl Schmitt's Political Theology II.

[11] Bucher summarizes in this part the main research question he raises in his *Habilitationschrift*: Bucher, Rainer. *Kirchenbildung in der Moderne. Eine Untersuchung der Konstitutionsprinzipien der Deutschen Katholischen Kirche im 20. Jahrhundert* (Stuttgart: Kohlhammer, 1988).

[12] See p. xviii

[13] See for example: Heschel, Susannah. *The Aryan Jesus. Christian Theologians and the Bible in Nazi Germany* (Princeton: Princeton University Press, 2010); Steigmann-Gall, Richard. *The Holy Reich. Nazi Conceptions of Christianity, 1919–1945* (Cambridge: Cambridge University Press, 2004); Gailus, Manfred. *Protestantismus und Nationalsozialismus. Studien zur nationalsozialistischen Durchdringung des protestantischen Sozialmilieus in Berlin* (Köln: Böhlau, 2001); Bergen, Doris. *Twisted Cross. The Christian Movement in the Third Reich* (North Carolina: North Carolina University Press, 1996); Ericksen, Robert P. *Theologians under Hitler* (New Haven: Yale University Press, 1985).

[14] See: Hobsbawm, Eric. *The Age of Extremes. 1914–1991* (London: Little Brown, 2009) pp. 109–141. On the role played by the Catholic Church during the rise of Nazism, see: p. 115.

[15] Hobsbawm, Eric. *The Age of Extremes. 1914–1991* (London: Little Brown, 2009) pp. 127–8.

[16] See in this book: p. xviii

[17] In Austria for example (*Bundesverfassungsgesetz, Verbotsgesetz §3*) the constitutions legally prohibits any form of re-engagement with National Socialism, propagation of Nazi propaganda or denial of the Holocaust. Between 1999 and 2004, 158 cases have been sentenced on the basis of this law.

[18] Reck, Norbert. ' " . . . Er verfolgt die Schuld der Väter und Söhnen und Enkel, an der dritten und vierten Generation" (Ex 34, 7)'. Nationalsozialismus, Holocaust und Schuld in den Augen dreier katholischer Generationen. In: Björn Krondorfer, Katharina von Kellenbach, Norbert Reck. *Mit Blick auf die Täter. Fragen an die deutsche Theologie nach 1945* (Gütersloh: Gütersloher Verlagshaus, 2006) pp. 171–225.

[19] Reck, Norbert. ' " . . . Er verfolgt die Schuld der Väter und Söhnen und Enkel, an der dritten und vierten Generation" (Ex 34, 7). Nationalsozialismus, Holocaust und Schuld in den Augen dreier katholischer Generationen'. In: Björn Krondorfer, Katharina von Kellenbach, Norbert Reck. *Mit Blick auf die Täter. Fragen an die deutsche Theologie nach 1945* (Gütersloh: Gütersloher Verlagshaus, 2006) p. 192.

[20] Reck, Norbert. ' " . . . Er verfolgt die Schuld der Väter und Söhnen und Enkel, an der dritten und vierten Generation" (Ex 34, 7).' p. 209.

[21] Reck, Norbert. ' " . . . Er verfolgt die Schuld der Väter und Söhnen und Enkel, an der dritten und vierten Generation" (Ex 34, 7).' pp. 213–14.

[22] In ths book, p. 122

[23] Voegelin, Eric. *The Political Religions* (Lewiston, NY: E. Mellen Press, 1986).

Part I

Framing the Matter

Chapter 1

'Hitler's Theology': What It Is and What It Is Not About

Hitler's project

National Socialism was something truly new: it was an amalgam of technical modernization and the promises of national collectivity and social equality, full of promises of aesthetic fascination and individual heroism that were fascinating for many people. National Socialism seemed to recombine the things which, according to many commentators at the time, had drifted apart at the latest during the forced wave of modernization of the Weimar Republic: individuality and collectivity, modernity and continuity with tradition, freedom (as opposed, for example, to stale Christianity) and bonds with past greatness. Above all, however, National Socialism promised the idyll of the *Volksgemeinschaft* based on notions of cultural familiarity and unity which created a sense of identity.

The fact that within a differentiated society such a project could only work through massive mechanisms of violence and annexation was clear from the beginning and was never hidden by the regime. The open propensity to violence against all those who refused to join in had become evident since, at the latest, the Reichstag fire at the end of February 1933 and the subsequent wave of arrests. The outright murder of inner and outer party rivals at the end of July/beginning of August 1934, legitimized shortly afterwards by the Catholic expert in constitutional law Carl Schmitt with due legal finesse ('The Führer is protecting the law,')[1] and the early incipient discrimination against Jewish Germans showed very quickly: those who did not belong to the *Volksgemeinschaft* according to Hitler, or did not want to belong to it, were first dismissed and soon after sent to be exterminated. Admittedly, for a long time many in Germany – and not just there – wanted to belong.[2]

The success of German National Socialism was basically exclusively Adolf Hitler's project. He enforced it with vigour and skill and did not give up on it until his death. The fact that, programmatically speaking, the 'phenomenon itself existed before Hitler was heard of, and would have continued to exist if Hitler had remained a "nobody of Vienna"', is held to be certain.[3] Its success, however, was purely with and through Hitler. This was due to the ruthless cunning with which Hitler won power as well as the specific colouring he gave the '*völkisch* Movement' within National Socialism.

However, this does not mean that everything that actually happened in the partially polyarchal structure and increasingly chaotic government of the Third Reich is immediately traceable to Hitler. Nor, in reverse, does it mean that everything that Hitler's project envisaged was actually carried out.[4] Admittedly, there can not have been much leeway for substantial deviation. 'Once head of state, Hitler's personalized "world-view" would serve as "guidelines for action" for policy-makers in all areas of the Third Reich.'[5] As Ian Kershaw writes:

> The very inflexibility and quasi-messianic commitment to an 'idea', a set of beliefs that were unalterable, simple, internally consistent and comprehensive, gave Hitler the strength of will and sense of knowing his own destiny that left its mark on all those who came into contact with him.[6]

Hitler never concealed what he wanted. On the contrary: apart from his ruthlessness, the only extraordinary thing about him was his rhetorical skill. Hitler repeatedly stated in public what he wanted and what he thought. There are many project descriptions for Hitler's project and these are the object of this study, especially their theological elements and the position of these within that project. In 1969, Eberhard Jäckel was the first to attempt to demonstrate the internal coherence of 'Hitler's Weltanschauung.'[7] Jäckel identifies the 'conquest of *Lebensraum* to the East' as well as the 'removal of the Jews', as Jäckel puts it, as Hitler's key concerns.[8] Thus, Hitler wanted to dispose of the currently 'decadent' social condition of the liberal and pluralist democracy that he denounced with complete hatred. Admittedly, the conservative fundamentalist Right reaching as far as the Church and, in a different manner, the radical Left were also radically critical of democracy. What distinguished him from either of these?

Like the Left and unlike the Right, Hitler rejected the reactionary restoration of pre-revolutionary conditions, be they those predating 1919 or even those prior to 1789. He believed in the irreversibility, even the desirability, of each respective revolution. Hitler was looking for a new, non-restorative and yet anti-pluralist social basis of integration. He wanted more than just the conservative restoration of premodern ordering structures. However, unlike the Left, he did not seek this basis of integration on a Marxist 'class base' but on the basis of an as yet fictitious construct, the 'Aryan race'.

The conceptual merging that constitutes the term 'National Socialism' already showcases the forward-pressing attempt to escape the political schema of 'Left-Right' in use since the French Revolution.[9] This moves Hitler into the proximity of his contemporaries, the theoreticians of the so-called Conservative Revolution. However, Hitler differs from them not only in the radicality of his thought, but above all in its concrete operational feasibility. The reactionary visions of the 'Conservative Revolution' could not be politically realized: they never moved beyond literary cultural effectiveness, and Hitler knew this all too well.

By integrating important elements of the post-feudal social programme of modernization into his project, Hitler prevented it from deteriorating into a simple conservative utopia. Hitler did not want to restore a lost pre-revolutionary paradise, utopias of the kind cultivated in Church circles.[10] He established connections with the Weimar Republic through the introduction, led by fascination, of new technologies, the programme of an industrial society based on continuous scientific and technical innovation, and key anti-conservative ideas such as equal opportunities and an increase in both vertical and horizontal social mobility – even to the point of egalitarian tendencies, as for example in the education system.[11] Primarily, he inherited the promises of happiness offered by modernity, including the promise of its technological producibility and social accessibility for all.

The foundation, the core of Hitler's political project, though, was a sharply racist anti-universalism. Hitler's project boils down to a racially defined 'Volksgemeinsschaft', inwardly characterised by 'harmonious' unity and outwardly characterised by belligerent heroism. For this community Hitler needed the 'Raum im Osten', and from this community members of 'inferior races' had to be removed, particularly the Jews, but also all those who opposed this project.

To Hitler's mind, this German or Aryan Volksgemeinschaft had been called to nothing less than world domination due to its racial superiority that manifests itself not least in its cultural superiority. For Hitler, the would-be painter, all this is grounded in and perhaps also motivated by[12] a cultural-aesthetic anti-modernism that trivialises the visual arts,[13] but also music,[14] to accord with the contemporary taste of the lower middle classes.

Hitler and the Churches

The Church did not want Hitler but it also did not stop him.[15] The Catholic Church did, for the most part, avoid the Nazification of its own structures and successfully secured areas for itself – albeit very limited in number – that eluded the rule of the party. This was grounded in the widespread antagonism within the Catholic Church up until 1933 – and especially within political Catholicism – towards the ethos, goals and methods of the NSDAP. Exceptions such as the rector of the Anima in Rome, Bishop Alois Hudal,[16] the infamous Abbot Schachleiter[17] as well as the so-called 'brown* priests'[18] did, in fact, remain exceptions.

---

* In German, the adjective 'brown' signifies the adjectival use of the term 'Nazi', that is, it signifies a particular political attitude. Unless part of a quotation and/or technical terms, 'brown' has been translated as 'Nazi'.

However, it seems equally indisputable that the Catholic Church did not seriously want to prevent the Nazification of social structures either in Germany or in Austria once Hitler had come to power. As a whole and under the leadership of its bishops, the Catholic Church never even attempted to prevent the consolidation of the National Socialist rule in the early years, let alone to overthrow it.

For the purposes of a differentiated concept of resistance,[19] the Catholic Church as a whole can be credited with having remained a 'rivalling centre of loyalty'. Regionally, there were also more or less spontaneous refusals organized by the Church and in rare cases active protest as well, but never any overt or subversive resistance that worked towards overthrowing National Socialism. Insofar as 'resistance' is taken to mean acts of resistance, there was, to be sure, resistance from Catholics. But there was no resistance on the part of the official leadership of the Catholic Church.

Yet from the consolidation of the regime in 1934 until well into the war, Catholics, too, were loyal, perhaps not necessarily to the party, but largely to the state. The indisputable 'early successes' of the regime (reduction of unemployment, the plebiscite in the Saarland 1936, occupation of the Rhineland 1936, Olympic Games 1936, remilitarization, successful prewar annexations right up to the war, annexation of Austria 1938) were effective with Catholics as well. Moreover, a critical political awareness of dictatorship as a form of government was not common within the Catholic community.

The reasons for this are manifold. Throughout the nineteenth century the Catholic Church had emphasized obedience to lawful authority in both its doctrine and its proclamations.[20] By contrast, other traditions from moral theology, such as the legitimacy of tyrannicide, never developed very far. The ecclesiastical magisterium of the nineteenth century had preached obedience and subordination as the prominent Catholic virtues in its defence against modern plurality and liberality. This extreme emphasis on the authority principle naturally promoted authoritarian state traditions, even seemed to justify them. Democracy and Liberalism were seen as opponents by large parts of the Catholic Church, rather than as a goal to be attained.

In addition, the 1930s saw a certain susceptibility to authoritarian regimes throughout the Church. In Italy and Spain the Church had openly acted as an ally of fascism and Franco respectively, and in Austria it acted as protector, even creative director, of the authoritarian corporate state. German National Socialism was clearly distinct from Romance fascism and even more distinct from the Austrian corporate state, which is why there was never a comparable alliance between Church and National Socialism. However, the Catholic Church's lack of defence against fascism internationally was a considerable millstone around the neck of the German Catholic Church.

The Reich Agreement of 1933 between Hitler and the Pope seemed to guarantee the protection of the vested interests of the ecclesiastical institutions. This safeguard of institutional integrity was seen to be paramount and ultimately sufficient.[21] Hitler's opponents in both of the large denominations were never more than a tiny minority. The majority, while by no means loving him, came to terms with him.

The evaluation of this fact still varies substantially today. This is not particularly surprising in as much as the context for evaluating historical facts, and even the context of their discovery, relies heavily on predetermined starting positions. It is not especially surprising that these horizons for evaluation should differ greatly with respect to an institution that itself acted on the basis of a high moral claim as well as, for a long period, the power to socially sanction and psychologically regulate subjects. Incidentally, these variations have not been least pronounced within theology and the Church.

The core of the disagreement centres on whether the evaluation of the behaviour of ecclesiastical agents should be based on the then dominant ecclesiology, which was highly institutionalized and apologetic – this would shed a more favourable light on ecclesiastical actions, at least in terms of morality. Or whether the evaluation should be based on the post-conciliar pastoral mission formulated by the Church, which was oriented more strongly towards human rights and saw the institution as the 'universal sacrament of salvation'. This makes the Church's erosion of solidarity with non-members, as well as, to a degree, with its own members (for example 'christened non-Aryans'), a fundamental failure in the face of its own message. From a historical as well as an individualist ethical perspective, the former seems likely; from a theological perspective, the latter. However, critical approaches do show that even though the 'post-conciliary', universalist position was not dominant at the time, it was still present, represented, for example, by Bishop Preysing[22] or the so-called Committee of Religious Orders (*Ordensausschuss*),[23] that is by exactly those people who represented an alternative to the official politics of the Bishops' Conference.[24]

The 'National Socialist cult'

The Church soon became aware of the fact that National Socialism was competing with it on its own grounds – the religious formation of life. The Church was especially concerned about the heavily anti-Christian, 'neo-pagan' tendencies that were particularly prominent in the early days of the National Socialist movement. Warnings of 'a new Weltanschauung to replace the Christian faith' had been issued,[25] especially because this new Weltanschauung did not remain purely theoretical but developed alternative religious practices, albeit not very successfully. The attempt of the National Socialists to immediately penetrate Christian domains – Christmas for example – remained fairly unsuccessful; essentially, it remained limited to their own core following. For instance, they never succeeded in a nationwide substitution of Christian Christmas carols

with National Socialist creations of sublimity stripped of all Christian reference[26] ('Hohe Nacht der klaren Sterne').[27]

The inverse proved much more successful: the importing of Christian and
non-Christian ritualistic traditions (consecrations, processions, pilgrimages,
commemorative services) into the exercise of National Socialist rule. The fact
that cultic stagings on various levels and of various types were essential to the
National Socialist technique of rule was recognized early on and has been
analyzed in detail in the past years.[28]

What was specifically National Socialist here was not only the monumen-
tality and the unrestrained desire for effect, but the radicalness with which
the newest technical instruments were employed for the cultic stagings. The
'light cathedrals' (*Lichtdom*) at the party rallies are spectacular examples of
the power and technical innovation of these stagings. On the eve of the fifth
day the nighttime honouring ceremony for the 'Political Leaders', that is the
lower and intermediary party functionaries, was scheduled. Ever since the
'light cathedral' had premiered at the '*Reichsparteitag des Willens*' in 1934, this
imaginary cathedral created by Albert Speer was considered the climax of
party rallies and an intense experience of the National Socialist liturgy.

At nightfall over 100,000 functionaries formed a close, brown block on
the Zeppelin Field at the party rally grounds in Nuremberg; in the stands
around them, the same number of spectators waited. A clarion call announced
Hitler – hundreds of red party flags, also illuminated, fluttered in the wind.
The colonnade of the main stand was indirectly lit from within; fires blazed on
the corner pillars of the stand.

Just as Hitler ascended the stand, the gigantic 'light cathedral' came into
being. Spaced at intervals of twelve metres, the entire field was lined with 130
flak spotlights that projected their light six to eight kilometres into the sky –
parallel to begin with and then, in a dramatic act of fusion, uniting to form a
cupola. One can imagine the overwhelming effect. After a moment's silence,
the 25,000 flags of all National Socialist local groups were carried onto the
field, along with gilded eagles on standards. This was followed by the honouring of the dead and the *Weihlied*, then Hitler gave a brief speech, there
were shouts of 'Heil' and the national anthem. And thus the minor National
Socialist functionary was initiated.

Incidentally, as sometimes happens with endeavours that are too grandi-
ose, there is an element of the ridiculous here. Albert Speer 'invented' the
'light cathedral' because unlike the disciplined, slim men of the SS and the
Wehrmacht, the Nazi functionaries 'had converted their small prebends into
sizable paunches' as Speer writes in his memoir, which is why he suggested having 'them march up in darkness'.[29]

Without a doubt, the National Socialists understood the power of the cultic
and the liturgical and National Socialism ruled not only through terror and
violence, but also through fascination and aesthetic seduction that could be

experienced firsthand. For its followers it unlocked intense experiences of a cultic nature in as much as it mediated the religious, through collective experiential orgies, as something primarily aesthetic. With this strategy it undermined both the enlightened critique of religion of the eighteenth and nineteenth centuries as well as the rationalism of Catholic theology and the Catholic Church as it fled into a pre-Enlightenment ghetto of Neoscholasticism.

National Socialism's liturgical-cultic competency – compacted, conserved and disseminated yet again in Leni Riefenstahl's *Triumph of the Will* from 1935 – was equally impressive and striking. Its connection to Hitler's theology is also evident, because it was Hitler who stood at the centre of most of these liturgies and when not staging them himself, monitored them meticulously. But above all, Hitler's liturgies were the liturgical celebratory side of his theology, staging it as a powerful experience. This raises the following question: What theology is celebrating its faith here? What faith is invested with aesthetic and ritualistic presence here?

'Hitler's religion'

This question must be distinguished from that of 'Hitler's religion.' The issue at hand is not Hitler's personal, deeply held religious beliefs, or even his personal religiosity in the sense of his religious practice.[30] Assertions about personally held beliefs or about the personal practice of faith – and these would have to be made were one really to talk about 'Hitler's religion' – are extraordinarily difficult to make and even more difficult to substantiate, especially for historical persons. For however you may define religion, these beliefs and practices concern the innermost of the human, his deepest convictions, his relation to the world and to the cosmos in general.

Admittedly, some evidence indicates that Hitler also personally believed what he wrote and said about God, Providence, faith, the German people as the chosen one and similar matters, that is, they were views he personally shared. The frequency as well as the downright uncanny constancy of his accordant declarations, for instance, is striking. They can be found from the early speeches of the so-called *Kampfzeit* through *Mein Kampf* up until his final writings and statements in the first few months of 1945.

Furthermore, what I try to reconstruct in the following as 'Hitler's theology' clearly became a guiding principle to the movement. The fact that Hitler fanatically continued to pursue the murder of European Jews when it had become clear even to him that this would destroy Germany and himself and a different deployment of the last resources – say for national defence – suggested itself, is as striking as it is in need of explanation.[31] This leads to the conclusion that the reasons behind his actions were independent of events and instead rooted in persistent convictions.

Certainly: Hitler also doubtlessly exploits religious practices and beliefs with some cynicism and cunningness. His appearances at the National Socialist mass liturgies, for example, are rehearsed and of cool rationality. On the other hand, Hitler clearly succumbs to his own performances and emphatically affirms the authenticity of the religious. It is well known that Hitler described himself as deistic, none other than Cardinal Faulhaber attested to this after his visit to the Obersalzberg on 4 November 1936: 'Without a doubt, the Reich Chancellor lives in the belief in God,'[32] Faulhaber wrote to the Bavarian bishops. Hitler's approach to concrete religious practices might hence best be called 'semi-exploitative'.

Hitler's theology directed the priorities of his actions. It never became official National Socialist doctrine: there were always also other, albeit related, concepts, for example from Himmler,[33] Ley[34] or Rosenberg.[35] They were certainly all racist, but they were distinct in their respective proximity to and distance from '*völkisch* neo-paganism', monotheism or generally the question of the relationship between rationality and faith. Himmler, for example, was a monotheist and simultaneously a follower of occult practices; Hitler was a monotheist and an opponent of all things occult; others really were polytheistic 'neo-pagans'.

Moreover, the NSDAP officially professed its faith in 'positive Christianity', whatever that was meant to be exactly. For Hitler himself his theology was a valid standard: time and again he returns to it, is guided by its fundamental ideas, and also publishes it. Even when reality proves to be completely different from what his theology had anticipated, he doesn't abandon it – if anything, he abandons himself and the German people. Instead of the path of apostasy, Hitler chooses the path of self – and, by intention at least, also that of world destruction – his words and deeds are in thorough agreement. Hitler acted in accordance with his theology: from a purely intrinsic perspective, there cannot be stronger proof of its personal relevance.

This study will examine which God this theology is speaking of and what commands this God issues. So it is not Hitler's personal religiosity, which would be difficult to determine, but the description of his political project and its theological structures of legitimation that will be reconstructed. For this can be verified, since Hitler spoke of it time and again.

National Socialism as 'political religion'

Now, contemporaries had already understood National Socialism as a whole to be a 'political religion',[36] and had thus attempted to understand it primarily from the perspective of religious studies. The first to opt for this approach to analyzing National Socialism was the emigrated Austrian philosopher and expert in constitutional law Erich Voegelin. In his study *Political Religions*[37] he classified these as political mass movements that sacralize the intramundane – such as the State, race or class – with the aim of bringing about an ideal intramundane state of affairs.

Voegelin argues that modern totalitarianisms represented secularized forms of formerly ecclesiastical, religious certainties. According to Voegelin's thesis, the collapse of classical ecclesiastic authority in modernity led to the development of intramundane religions that replace a transcendental god with immanent phenomena which, for the followers of these 'political religions', take on precisely the religious significance formerly held by religious beliefs.

So for Voegelin, political religions embody doctrines of salvation that, like the classical religions, explain the whole of history. Unlike them, however, political religions imagine the ultimate aim of history as achievable within history itself. This achievability then justifies absolute violence, not as an eruption of raw passion, but as the cool execution of a recognised logic, as 'cleansing' and 'liberation'. Political religions are hence not understood as a relapse into previous atrocities but as the expression of a new, immanent, but absolute faith.

Voegelin's approach has been critically debated from the start. The objections to Voegelin boil down to a criticism of his concept of religion, which, ultimately, encompasses only the purely immanent as well as including absolute cruelty – even the atrocious. Furthermore, in application to National Socialism, it assumes that the latter was a reasonably cohesive and self-contained system.

Precisely these three premises put forward by Voegelin – that it is useful to also speak of purely immanent religions, that religions encompass not only the highest but also the most atrocious, and that National Socialism, under Hitler at least, represents a relatively coherent, albeit primitive, system – today should seem more plausible again. The totalitarian political projects of the twentieth century can be understood as risk-taking versions of modernity's enlightened separation of religion and politics in as much as they reverse this separation; that is, they resacralize the political, only this time from the now independent sphere of the political. This will be returned to later.

However, the present study's approach is in a sense more modest. It is not concerned with carrying forward Voegelin's universalist history but with analysing Hitler's texts in terms of their theological categories.

On the employed concept of theology

Admittedly, to speak of 'theology' with respect to Hitler is provocative. It provokes theologians because they suddenly find themselves in close proximity to that which could not be any more heinous. It also, however, provokes Christians and other believers because what they believe in, God, is seemingly moved into close proximity with one of the worst criminals in the history of the world.

Now theologians know that 'theology' is not a protected term and that there have been and continue to be many highly distinctive theologies. After long centuries during which the Christian Church determined what theology was and could be, the field of 'theologies' gradually extended beyond Christianity during the eighteenth century, initially for scholars, but during the nineteenth century throughout society more broadly. Today, after the definite end of any ecclesiastical sanctioning power and the ultimate release into religious self-determination,[38] the 'theological field' is broad, open and multifaceted, even though the Christian Church continues to hold a strong institutional position.

Moreover, believers can learn from history that religion and its theoretical concepts are neither harmless nor nonviolent. If anything, the opposite holds true:

> The uncritical association of religion with goodness is directly negatived by plain facts. Religion can be, and has been, the main instrument for progress. But if we survey the whole race, we must pronounce that generally it has not been so.[39]

It has even been said that '[r]eligion is the last refuge of human savagery.'[40]

The current remilitarization of religion in specific areas of the world furthermore demonstrates that this is by no means a phenomenon of the past. On the contrary, religion is back and it shows its ugly face next to its benign countenance time and again: hypocrisy, uncharitableness and violence. In any case, the liberal illusion of progressing towards a globally secularized world community of harmless and peaceful individualized religious practice has faded. Theology and religion are neither reserved to Christianity nor are they innately good things. So, to speak of 'Hitler's theology' presupposes that the term theology is not reserved for a discourse on and thought about God that one can agree with, but for *all discourse about God,* and also, especially, its consequences.

The *second* premise is that theology does not only signify scholastic theology. Hitler did not engage in this, even though he could impress even his academic interlocutors time and again with his notorious half-knowledge and even though, as will be shown later, in his opinion his theology was founded in science, even natural science. Hitler's theology does, however, show traces of a certain internal consistency and coherence despite all its vulgarity and primitiveness.

It has become somewhat unusual today not to limit the term 'theology' either to discourse about God that allows agreement or to scholastic discourse on God. However, this has not always been the case. In a certain sense, it was exactly the other way round in the beginning of Christianity's history. For instance, early Christianity expressly rejected the term 'theology'. It can not be found anywhere

in the New Testament and the Early Fathers used the term in a negatively critical sense. As it was understood in the Greek environment the term was simply
unacceptable for Christian reflections on faith. Its proximity to non-Christian,
mythic-cultic contexts prevented Christianity's early theologians from relating
the term to themselves and the issues that concerned them.[41]

In the following, however, theology is understood literally as meaning 'discourse on God', and this corresponds with today's general understanding:
discourse on God with the option for individual relevance, the potential for
personal consequences to the point of speaking to God in prayer. For it is precisely this that one can not deny Hitler.

Of course, Hitler is neither a Christian nor an academic theologian, but
he announces his political project in the name of a god, and he does this
from the start of his public orations up until his last documented comments.
The theology of these pronouncements can be surveyed. Hitler's texts embody
a genuine theological discourse in the sense outlined above. Unfortunately,
they embody more than just an ineffective private mythology.

Only rhetoric?

The fact that it was key to Hitler's rhetoric[42] to employ the stylistic devices of religious discourse[43] as well as theological terminology was also noted early on. As
early as 1939 Kenneth Burke, the American communication theorist, observed
the following in his brilliant essay on 'The Rhetoric of Hitler's "Battle"': 'the
patterns of Hitler's thought are a bastardized or caricatured version of religious thought'[44] and 'Hitler appeals by relying upon a bastardization of fundamentally religious patterns of thought.'[45] Incidentally, the *media format* of the
dissemination of Hitler's speeches was conceptualized in theological categories by the National Socialist propaganda itself: 'What the Church building is
for religion, broadcasting will be for the cult of the new state.' Broadcasting
services were 'now no longer broadcasts** in the physical and technical sense,
but finally in a spiritual sense. Everybody involved in broadcasting services
carries the National Socialist mission, is propagandist and apostle of the idea,'
explained Eugen Hadamovsky who was 'National Programming Director'
(*Reichssendeleiter*) from 1933 to 1942.[46]

Above all, in the late 1960s the Austrian cultural historian and journalist
Friedrich Heer identified in great detail the theological origins of many of
the hackneyed phrases of Hitler's discourse.[47] Of course, the chiliastic back-
ground[48] of much of Hitler's terminology – for example, the 'Third Reich',
which he viewed with increasing suspicion – had been conspicuous. Hitler's

---

** The German term here is 'Sendung', which is ambiguous bearing both broadcasting
and, crucially in this instance, religious connotations of the Christian mission.

faith in science, however, certainly makes it especially advisable not to over-estimate this chiliastic influence on Hitler – Hitler abandoned the term 'Third Reich' after 1933 precisely because of its 'enraptured' implications.[49]

Despite substantial engagement with Hitler's rhetoric, the blatant theological component of Hitlerian discourse has long been read as just that: rhetorical strategy. However, Hitler's theological terminology shapes founding principles of his thought and his political project. The inspection of Hitler's texts, in any case, shows that Hitler's discourse is continuously laced with theological terminology throughout all phases of his political biography. They are not simply rhetorical, they are central and constitutive.

Theological elements are to be expected above all in three places in Hitlerian discourse: first, where Hitler deals with the Church, that is, where he defines his plan in opposition to the traditional carriers of theological responsibility; secondly, also where he deals with the genuinely religious tradition of his own movement, that is, the *völkisch* religiosity; thirdly, though, and centrally, those parts of the Hitlerian discourse are to be located, where he conceptualizes and legitimizes his own project through theological terms.

Notes

[1]   Schmitt, 'Der Führer schützt das Recht'. On Schmitt from the perspective of the 'New Political Theology' (*Neue Politische Theologie*): Manemann, *Carl Schmitt*. See also: Wacker, *Katholische Verschärfung*; H. Meier, *Lehre Carl Schmitts*.

[2]   Among other things because it promised advancement, riches and booty as Aly shows in *Hitlers Volksstaat*.

[3]   Kershaw, *Hitler I*, 134.

[4]   A heavy controversy broke out in the mid-1980s between 'revisionists' or 'functionalists' who were oriented towards structuralist historiography (*histoire de structures* as developed by Braudel) (Broszat, Mommsen, Hüttenberger) and 'programmologists' or 'intentionalists' who held fast to the notion of Hitler's decisive role (Fest, Bracher, Hildebrand, Hillgruber). The dispute between Hildebrand and Mommsen carried out under the title 'Nationalsozialismus oder Hitlerismus?' is reprinted in: Wippermann, *Kontroversen um Hitler*, 199–216. On the history of research here see: Schreiber, *Hitler*; for a somewhat brisk judgment: Lukacs, *Hitler*. A brief but very instructive literature review of the vast debate on Hitler is given by Kershaw, *Hitler I*, xix–xxx, 597–603. For an introduction to the Hitler phenomenon next to Kershaw's biography, Haffner, *Anmerkungen* is (still) especially to be recommended. See also: Haffner, *Geschichte eines Deutschen*.

[5]   Kershaw, *Hitler I*, 244.

[6]   Ibid., 243.

[7]   Jäckel, *Hitlers Weltanschauung*. Kershaw also comments on the 'internal coherence (given the irrational premises)' (*Hitler I*, 244).

8 See also: Wippermann, *Der konsequente Wahn*. In this context the question needs to be considered of how far Hitler's discourse can be interpreted as a general attempt to restore the homogeneity of social discourse, for example under the category of 'common sense', that had been lost in modernity in order to bring about a counterbalance to the individual sciences that were no longer integrable and of which Hitler, as is well known, had, in places, a striking knowledge of details which he could, to all intents and purposes, assemble into a coherent whole on the basis of what has in the relevant literature been diagnosed as his 'unscientific-ness' ['*Unwissenschaftlichkeit*'].

9 See: Breuer, *Anatomie der Konservativen Revolution*; Sontheimer, *Antidemokratisches Denken*; Sieferle, 'Die Konservative Revolution und das "Dritte Reich"'. Kershaw's analysis can be endorsed: 'The foundations of a rounded anti-democratic ideology, an antithesis to Weimar, were established not in the primitive beer-table discussions of *völkisch* "thinkers" and "philosophers", but by neo-conservative writers, publicists and intellectuals such as Wilhelm Stapel, Max Hildebert Boehm, Moeller van den Bruck, Othmar Spann, and Edgar Jung' (Kershaw, *Hitler I*, 136).

10 Cf.: Breuning, *Vision des Reiches*; Ruster, *Verlorene Nützlichkeit*; Bröckling, *Katholische Intellektuelle*.

11 Which then also enabled the fatal continuity of elites from Weimar to National Socialism and beyond. Cf.: Frei, *Hitlers Eliten*. On Germany's interwar political and cultural state see: Kluge, *Weimarer Republik*; Schulze, *Weimar*; Marcowitz, *Weimarer Republik*; Winkler, '*Weimar 1918–1933*'; Cancik, *Religions- und Geistesgeschichte*.

12 Cf.: Hamann, *Hitler's Vienna*, esp. 60–85.

13 Cf.: Schuster, *Nationalsozialismus und 'Entartete Kunst'*.

14 Cf.: Prieberg, *Musik im NS-Staat*.

15 From the varied and in places controversial literature on the problematic issue of the Catholic Church and National Socialism see: Bendel, *Katholische Schuld*; Hürten, *Deutsche Katholiken*; Gotto/Repgen, *Die Katholiken und das Dritte Reich*; Scholder, *Die Kirchen und das Dritte Reich*, vols. I and II; Volk, *Katholische Kirche und Nationalsozialismus*. See also: Hummel, *Katholizismusforschung*.

16 Burkard, 'Alois Hudal'; M. Langer, 'Alois Hudal'; Liebmann, 'Bischof Hudal'.

17 Bleistein, 'Abt Alban Schachleiter OSB'.

18 Spicer, 'Gespaltene Loyalität'.

19 Following on from Peter Hüttenberger's thoughts in the context of the so-called Bavarian Project ['*Bayern-Projekt*'] (cf. Hüttenberger, 'Widerstandsbegriff') and further developing the 'resistance' concept presented there (cf. the introduction to the first volume of that research project, written by Martin Broszat: Broszat/Fröhlich/Wiesemann, *Bayern in der NS-Zeit*, vol. I, 11–19) a scale of four forms of deviating behaviour was distinguished along the parameters of the respective degrees of the private and public nature of the act of resistance as well as its – partial or general – scope of criticism of the system. This scale spans (a) the purely private and partial nonconformity (b) the passive refusal of some elements of demands made by the ruling elite (c) the active, albeit still regional public protest and (d) the actual resistance aimed at overthrowing the regime.

20 Cf.: Leugers, 'Positionen der Bischöfe'; Leugers, 'Adolf Kardinal Bertram'; Köhler, 'Adolf Kardinal Bertram'.

21 On the Concordat see: Volk, *Reichskonkordat*; Scholder, *Die Kirchen und das Dritte Reich*, vol. I. On the discussion of Scholder's explosive hypothesis of a causal link between the Enabling Act [*Ermächtigungsgesetz*] and the Concordat see: Repgen, 'Entstehung der Reichkonkordats-Offerte'; also: Scholder, 'Vorgeschichte des Reichskonkordats'; a summary of the controversy from Repgen's perspective in: 'Repgen, Reichskonkordats-Kontroversen'.

22 See: Knauft, *Konrad von Preysing*.

23 See: Leugers, *Gegen eine Mauer*. Also see the collection: Rösch, *Kampf gegen den Nationalsozialismus*.

24 Incidentally, this issue presents a remarkable crosswise argument from the perspective of argumentative theory: Conservative historians operate with a more historically relativist ecclesiology such as really was not represented at the time, while critical researchers take a more systematically normative look at the Church.

25 Thus reads the pastoral statement released by the Bavarian bishops on 10 February 1931 (Stasiewski, *Akten deutscher Bischöfe*, vol. I, 806–9, 806); similar instructions and directives were issued by the ecclesiastical provinces of Cologne, Paderborn and the Upper Rhine.

26 Even the Greater Germany Broadcasting Service's [*Großdeutscher Rundfunk*] famous Europe-wide Christmas hookup on 24 December, the 'Christmas musical request show' [*Weihnachtswunschkonzert*], could not avoid Christian songs such as 'Silent Night' and 'O Du fröhliche', even though 'Hohe Nacht der klaren Sterne' also figured in the programme. Cf.: Institut für Zeitgeschichte, *Dokumentation Obersalzberg* (CD). The 'musical request programme' for the Wehrmacht had developed out of the 'Winter Relief Programme Musical Request Show [*Wunschkonzert für das Winterhilfswerk*] and served one purpose above all: 'uniting eighty million people in a grand community experience'. 'Anybody who should listen to such a musical request programme knows how people and Wehrmacht feel joined together as a single, large family' (Berndt, 'Vorwort', 8).

27 Gajek, ' "Hohe Nacht der klaren Sterne" '. Also see the entries on 'nationalsozialistische Weihnacht' in: Faber/Gajek, *Politische Weihnacht*.

28 Cf. e.g.: Karow, *Deutsches Opfer*; Karow, 'Konstruktion und Funktion nationalsozialistischer Mythenbildung'; Behrenbeck, *Kult um die toten Helden*; Reichelt, *Das Braune Evangelium*; Reichel, *Der schöne Schein*; Ogan/Weiss, *Faszination und Gewalt*; Dröge/Müller, *Macht der Schönheit*; Bärsch, 'Das Erhabene'; Becker, ' "Liturgie" im Dienst der Macht'. From older literature see: Gamm, *Der braune Kult*; Vondung, *Magie und Manipulation*. On the 'Hitler Myth': Kershaw, *The 'Hitler Myth'*.

29 Speer, *Inside the Third Reich*, 58.

30 This terminological imprecision is one of the book's many weaknesses: Hesemann, *Hitlers Religion*. Unfortunately, it is not always reliable in its facts as well as locating Hitler in too close proximity to *völkisch* religiosity. Significantly more valuable and also closer to my own approach both in terms of content and methodology are C.-E. Bärsch's studies. Bärsch already published an instructive

study of Goebbels quite a while ago (Bärsch, *Erlösung und Vernichtung*) and more recently presented a broadly researched study of Hitler, Goebbels, Eckart and Rosenberg (Bärsch, *Politische Religion*, on Hitler cf. esp. 271–319). I share Bärsch's view 'that for Hitler the decisive reason for being able to define and having to produce the identity of the German people was his specific faith in God and the divine substance of the Aryan race'(*Politische Religion*, 14). As a political scientist, Bärsch emphasizes the political consequences of Hitler's 'political religion' while the present study seeks to elaborate the internal architecture of Hitler's theology. Considerably more superficial in its analysis and all too brisk in its evaluation of already existing research: Rissmann, *Hitlers Gott*.

[31] Hitler was aware of the need to legitimize the prioritizing of the extermination of the Jews and justified it to the military: cf. Kershaw, *Hitler*, vol. II, 636–7.

[32] Volk, *Akten Kardinal Michael von Faulhabers*, vol. II, 194.

[33] Cf.: Wegener, *Himmler*; Ackermann, *Himmler*.

[34] On Ley: Smelser, *Robert Ley*.

[35] Cf. Bärsch, *Politische Religion*, 192–271.

[36] See Cancik, ' "Wir sind jetzt eins" ', 13–19. The discussion of this problem has been regaining momentun for a while now. See Ley/Schoeps, *Nationalsozialismus*, and Maier, *'Totalitarismus'*. On the religious dimension of the National Socialist ideology even during the Empire: Walkenhorst, 'Nationalismus als "politische Religion" '. Within the Church the religious valence of National Socialism was perceived from a significantly askew perspective in the post-war period. The key interpretive category for this was the concept of 'apostasy'. Cf. e.g. Künneth, *Der große Abfall*; also see: Bücker, *Schulddiskussion*, and the contributions by Metz, Fuchs, Boschki and Bendel-Maier in Bendel, *Katholische Schuld*.

[37] Voegelin, *Political Religions* [1938].

[38] Cf.: Bucher, *Provokation der Krise*; Gabriel, *Religiöse Individualisierung*.

[39] Whitehead, *Religion in the Making*, 37–8. Cf.: Maier, *Doppelgesicht*.

[40] Ibid.

[41] Cf.: Bayer/Peters, 'Art. Theologie'.

[42] On Hitler's rhetoric see: Burke, 'The Rhetoric of Hitler's "Battle" ' (originally published 1939); Grieswelle, *Propaganda der Friedlosigkeit* (esp. 43–63: 'Die Predigt eines politischen Glaubens'). Grieswelle 'concludes that Hitler's rhetoric can best be understood as the sermon of a political religion' (183). Cf. also: Grieswelle, *Rhetorik und Politik* (esp. 105–34: 'The Rhetoric of Political Religions'). An overview is available in Dyck, *Rhetorik im Nationalsozialismus*.

[43] The exemplary analysis of a speech by Hitler from the perspective of religious studies is available in: Cancik, ' "Wir sind jetzt eins" ', 13–48.

[44] Burke, 'Rhetoric of Hitler's "Battle" ', 199.

[45] Ibid., 219.

[46] Quoted in: Schmölders, 'Stimme des Bösen', 683.

[47] Next to Heer, *Der Glaube des Adolf Hitler*, see also: Heer, *Gottes erste Liebe*. Bärsch, *Politische Religion*, 271, rightly points out that 'the Catholic journalist Heer's solid studies hadn't (and still haven't) been received enough attention in the academic community.'

[48] On the rise of the chiliastically laden term 'Third Reich' in the 1920s including its predecessors in nineteenth-century philosophy of history see: Sieferle, 'Die

Konservative Revolution und das "Dritte Reich"'; Vondung, *Apokalypse in Deut-schland*; Maurer, 'Chiliasmus und Gesellschaftsreligion'; Rhodes, *Hitler Movement*; Cohn, *Ringen um das Tausendjährige Reich*.

[49] Sieferle, 'Konservative Revolution und das "Dritte Reich"', 201, notes that Hitler forbade the use of the term in 1939, albeit to no avail: Hitler did not want to appropriate this version of what was essentially a Christian theology of history just as much as he distanced himself from the 'mysticism' of the 'Conservative Revolution' in general.

Chapter 2

Hitler's Theology and the Catholic Church

Role model: What Hitler wanted to learn from the Church

Hitler courted the Church as much as he fought it in its role as a rivalling centre of loyalty.[1] In his writings and speeches, though, Hitler not only concerned himself with the Church in a topical and thus tactical context, but also from an analytical and hence absolutely fundamental perspective. Hitler is thus trying to shape his own political project in contrast to the Christian Church, but also partially in identification with it. To his mind, churches are primarily models for the social organization of religion, that is, something that he understands first and foremost as a 'Weltanschauung' – just like National Socialism.

Be they approving or critical, Hitler's considerations testify to an intense effort to distance himself from the Church. They also attest, incidentally, to Hitler's capacity for learning, which should not be underestimated. He fights the Church as a rival social organization, but he also wants to learn from it. Primarily, his interest in the Church is analytically motivated. Hitler examines the Church's constitutive principles, criticizes its beliefs and yet is also especially fascinated by the Catholic Church's ability to have organized and asserted itself over the centuries.

Again and again, Hitler delimits his own project of a racially defined *Volksgemeinschaft* in connection with as well as in contrast to the past and the present of the Christian Church. A clear trajectory from early admiration to increasingly intense critique is discernible throughout this process. Hitler's positive appraisal of the Church as a model for a successful organization that shaped a Weltanschauung can be identified from early on. As is to be expected, this is especially true in the comments and writings of the so-called *Kampfzeit*. It was at this time especially that references to other historically successful organizations which had negotiated the demands of standardization and pre-democratic legitimization seemed to suggest themselves.

The Church's claim to totality

Above all, Hitler admires Christianity's ability to assert itself on the basis of its ideological intransigence. This admiration can be found as early as in a text from the year 1922. The 'refusal to compromise', the repudiation of any 'alliance with so-called similar ideas', had, according to Hitler, given Christianity 'this outrageous power.' And further in a NSDAP bulletin from 26 April 1922: 'The greatest power in this world does not reside in work groups, but in the blind faith in the rightness of one's own goal and one's right to fight for this goal.'[2]

This argument can be found in almost identical form in *Mein Kampf*:

The greatness of every powerful organisation which embodies a creative idea lies in the spirit of religious devotion and intolerance with which it stands out against all others, because it has an ardent faith in its own right. If an idea is right in itself and, furnished with the fighting weapons I have mentioned, wages war on this earth, then it is invincible and persecution will only add to its internal strength. The greatness of Christianity did not arise from attempts to make compromises with those philosophical opinions of the ancient world which had some resemblance to its doctrine, but in the unrelenting and fanatical proclamation and defence of its own teaching.[3]

Christianity, according to Hitler,

was not content with erecting an altar of its own. It had first to destroy the pagan altars. It was only in virtue of this passionate intolerance that an apodictic faith could grow up. And intolerance is an indispensable condition for the growth of such a faith.[4]

In a speech given to teachers in Nuremberg, Hitler argues that 'Christianity won out not because it received a numerical majority, but because it received the majority of energies.' It is precisely this that provides the evidence for his optimistic outlook on the future of the then still insignificant NSDAP.

If I know a process, by which I can extract valuable people from a State, when the strongest have been extracted and appear in concentrated fashion at a particular point in time, then there is a new movement. That is what I had in mind when I began the formation of a new organisation,

said Hitler in this speech of 8 December 1928.[5]

Hitler does not just draw phenomenological parallels between the National Socialist Weltanschauung and Christianity's ability to assert itself, though. Rather, he explicitly justifies the National Socialist claim to totality by appealing to the necessity of warding off the antecedent Judaeo-Christian totalitarianism. For, according to Hitler,

A philosophy of life which is inspired by an infernal spirit of intolerance can only be set aside by a doctrine that is advanced in an equally ardent spirit and fought for with as determined a will and which is itself a new idea, pure and absolutely true.

Hitler continues by arguing that,

Each one of us to-day may regret the fact that the advent of Christianity was the first occasion on which spiritual terror was introduced into the much freer ancient world, but the fact cannot be denied that ever since then the world is pervaded and dominated by this kind of coercion and that violence is broken only by violence and terror by terror. Only then can a new regime be created by means of constructive work. *Political parties are prone to enter compromises; but a Weltanschauung never does this. A political party is inclined to adjust its teachings with a view to meeting those of its opponents, but a Weltanschauung proclaims its own infallibility.*[6]

So while to Hitler it may be 'a thousandfold true' that 'such fanaticism and intolerance are typical symptoms of Jewish mentality' this is also precisely why the National Socialist Weltanschauung must

imperiously deman[d] its own recognition as unique and exclusive and a complete transformation in accordance with its views throughout all the branches of public life. It can never allow the previous state of affairs to continue in existence by its side.[7]

In one of his later monologues, held on 4 April 1942 in the Führer headquarters, Hitler finally draws parallels between the exclusive adulation of a single God in Christianity, and the anti-universalist limitation of human rights to the German people in his own political project. According to Hitler, just as Christianity is 'most fanatical, most exclusionist, and most intolerant in the orientation of love towards the *one* God it has identified,' so 'all the love' of an 'unspoilt' National Socialist 'ruling class [should] be reserved *exclusively* for its own *Volksgenossen.*' Christianity is 'a good teacher' in this respect. Just as the former adores its God, 'the German elites must fanatically, exclusively, and intolerantly direct all their affection towards the hard-working German *Volksgenosse* who loyally and honestly fulfils his duty towards the entirety.'[8]

This misjudgement of Christian monotheism's universalist consequences is characteristic of Hitler's theology. The one and only God of the Judaeo-Christian tradition is precisely not the God of a single people: His commandments, first and foremost to love one's neighbour, fundamentally subvert any attempt at regionalizing it to a particular group of people, let alone a racial nation.

Dogma as a strategy of giving shape to diffuse elements

Hitler, quick to learn from the Church, now also formulates an explicit theory of dogma. For him, dogmas crystallize the intolerance necessary for successful religions and Weltanschauungen. It is only the dogma that ties together and concretizes the diffuse religiosity of the individual; only the dogma makes it predicable and hence politically potent.

Hitler argues that the '*völkisch* Weltanschauung' works in a similar manner. He draws parallels between the intellectual and social concretization and formation offered by his own project – a party based on a particular Weltanschauung, fit for action – and the function of the Church and its dogmas in the face of vague religious feeling.

A longer quotation from *Mein Kampf* exemplifies this:

> Without a clearly defined belief, the religious feeling would not only be worthless for the purposes of human existence but even might contribute towards a general disorganization, on account of its vague and multifarious tendencies.
>
> What I have said about the word 'religious' can also be applied to the term *völkisch*. This word also implies certain fundamental ideas. Though these ideas are very important indeed, they assume such vague and indefinite forms that they cannot be estimated as having a greater value than mere opinions, until they become constituent elements in the structure of a political party. *For in order to give practical force to the ideals that grow out of a Weltanschauung and to answer the demands which area logical consequence of such ideals, mere sentiment and inner longing are of no practical assistance, just as freedom cannot be won by a universal yearning for it. No. Only when the idealistic longing for independence is organized in such a way that it can fight for its ideal with military force, only then can the urgent wish of a people be transformed into a potent reality.*
>
> [. . .]If an abstract conception of a general nature is to serve as the basis of a future development, then the first prerequisite is to form a clear understanding of the nature and character and scope of this conception. For only on such a basis can a movement be founded which will be able to draw the necessary fighting strength from the internal cohesion of its principles and convictions. From general ideas a political programme must be constructed and a general Weltanschauung must receive the stamp of a definite political faith. [. . .]
>
> To take abstract and general principles, derived from a Weltanschauung which is based on a solid foundation of truth, and transform them into a militant community whose members have the same political faith – a community which is precisely defined, rigidly organized, of one mind and

one will – such a transformation is the most important task of all; for the possibility of successfully carrying out the idea is dependent on the successful fulfilment of that task. Out of the army of millions who feel the truth of these ideas, and even may understand them to some extent, *one man* must arise. This man must have the gift of being able to expound general ideas in a clear and definite form, and, from the world of vague ideas shimmering before the minds of the masses, he must formulate principles that will be as clear/cut and firm as granite. He must fight for these principles as the only true ones, until a solid rock of common faith and common will emerges above the troubled waves of vagrant ideas.[9]

To Hitler's mind it is then certain that without 'dogmatic principles [. . .] this human world of ours would be inconceivable without the practical existence of religious belief' and neither would a politically powerful Weltanschauung. 'The great masses of a nation are not composed of philosophers. For the masses of the people, especially faith is absolutely the only basis of a moral outlook on life.'[10]

Whether as a tactical move or as a result of his not yet fully overcome personal devotion, in *Mein Kampf* Hitler still concedes that the Church as it actually exists will continue to fulfil its role as religion that is given form through dogma. 'The various substitutes,' argues Hitler, 'have not shown any results that might warrant us in thinking that they might usefully replace the existing denominations,' even despite the fact that 'the attack on the dogmatic principles underlying ecclesiastical teaching increased steadily in violence.'[11]

But Hitler is not primarily interested in the plausibility of the content of these dogmas or the standardizations entailed by the contemporary Church. His interest is in the more formal aspects and is generally directed at the operative mechanisms that concretize and discipline diffuse elements in the process of building communities around a Weltanschauung. In relation to this, Hitler compares three very different areas that require concretization and standardization: the State, the Church, and the personal biography.

Hitler says,

Now the place which general custom fills in everyday life corresponds to that of general laws in the State and dogma in religion. The purely spiritual idea is of itself a changeable thing that may be subjected to endless interpretations. It is only through dogma that it is given a precise and concrete form without which it could not become a living faith. Otherwise the spiritual idea would never become anything more than a mere metaphysical concept, or rather a philosophical opinion.

And in consequence, the following holds true: 'But if religious teaching and religious faith were once accepted by the broad masses [. . .], then the absolute authority of the doctrines of faith would be the foundation of all practical effort.'[12]

Thus, in *Mein Kampf,* Hitler understands the sharply anti-modernist, defensive stance of the contemporary Church, especially the Catholic Church,[13] as the expression of a clever and consistent knowledge economy. For Hitler, the necessity of such a restrictive knowledge economy follows immediately from the concept of dogma. For even though 'sometimes, and often quite unnecessarily, [the Catholic Church's] dogmatic system is in conflict with the exacting sciences and with scientific discoveries, it is not disposed to sacrifice a syllable of its teachings.' That is to say, the Church

> has rightly recognized that its powers of resistance would be weakened by introducing greater or less doctrinal adaptations to meet the temporary conclusions of science, which in reality are always vacillating. And thus it holds fast to its fixed and established dogmas which alone can give to the whole system the character of a faith. And that is the reason why it stands firmer to-day than ever before.[14]

But at this early point in time Hitler also recognizes the following: in order for religious dogmas or, as the case may be, dogmas related to a Weltanschauung, to have the desired function of concretization and formation, their actual immutability is less important. As Hitler realizes, keeping hold of something too rigidly once it has been formulated can erode the plausibility of its claim to cognitive validity. It is, however, necessary always to maintain the perception of continuity in those to whom the propagation is addressed.

Hitler suggests that '[h]ere again the Catholic Church has a lesson to teach us.' 'For would it be possible to inspire people with blind faith in the truth of a doctrine if doubt and uncertainty are encouraged by continual alterations in its external formulation?' But Hitler is aware of the necessity of flexibility, he doesn't forget to incorporate a hermeneutic buffer with respect to his own political project: 'The essentials of a teaching,' Hitler says earlier, 'must never be looked for in its external formulas, but always in its inner meaning. And this meaning is unchangeable.'[15] This is why to Hitler's mind, 'there is only one doctrine. *People and Fatherland*' and '[i]t is from this standpoint that everything must be examined and turned to practical uses or else discarded. Thus a theory can never become a mere dead dogma since everything will have to serve the practical ends of everyday life.'[16]

Later, Hitler will accuse the Church of clinging to scientifically untenable dogmas and treat his own National Socialist 'dogmas' quite flexibly, while always maintaining continuity with a few key assumptions, such as the hypothesis of the racially determined individual.[17]

Organizational-operative problem-solving

But for Hitler, the Church is not only an object lesson for his own project because of its claim to totality and its achievements in the use of dogma to concretize and standardize what is in itself, after all, vague religious feeling. Hitler was also always especially interested in organizational-operative problem-solving. He was particularly fascinated by the Catholic Church's handling of a precarious problem for any non-democratically organized social system: the recruitment of elites, including the concrete mechanisms of leadership selection and succession.[18]

'Two constitutions,' claims Hitler in his table talks in the Führer headquarters on 3 December 1942, had 'stood the test of time: (a) the papacy, and this despite numerous crises' nor does he forget to add, 'despite a distinctly mad spiritual foundation purely due to the terrific organisation of the Church.' And '(b) the Venetian constitution which, through the organisation of its leadership, enabled the small republican city state to rule the entire eastern Mediterranean.'[19]

Hitler detects one of the reasons for the success of the papacy in the Catholic Church's very deft avoidance of the essentially unavoidable critique of authority concomitant with any decision process regarding leadership positions. This is achieved by keeping these processes, especially the election of the pope, strictly secret. Thus it prevents the inevitable conflicts arising within the upper echelons from becoming fully public.

'The basic principle for the election of the Führer', continues Hitler, should therefore be 'that all discussion amongst voters be prohibited during the voting process'. The

> procedure of electing the Führer should not happen under the eyes of the people, but behind closed doors. After all, the people didn't know what was going on behind the scenes of the papal election, either. Purportedly, the cardinals once even came to blows. This is why they have since simply been locked away for the duration of the electoral process.

Even if a form of government that bore this in mind

> might not last forever, it would surely last for 200 to 300 years. For it would be founded on rational considerations, while the organisation of the Catholic Church, that is a thousand years old, is built on a foundation of nonsense.[20]

To Hitler, 'the Catholic Church presents an instructive example' in yet another aspect of the recruitment of elites. 'Clerical celibacy forces the Church,' writes Hitler in *Mein Kampf*, 'to recruit its priests not from their own ranks but progressively from the masses of the people.' And this is seen as

> the cause of the inexhaustible vigour which characterizes that ancient institution. For by thus unceasingly recruiting the ecclesiastical dignitaries from the lower classes of the people, the Church is enabled not only to maintain the contact of instinctive understanding with the masses of the population but also to assure itself of always being able to draw upon that fund of energy which is present in this form only among the popular masses. Hence the surprising youthfulness of that gigantic organism, its mental flexibility, and its iron will-power.[21]

Demonstrably, Hitler's partial respect for the Church is a consequence of his analysis of its internal constitutional principles as perceived by him. In its role as an organization that shaped a Weltanschauung which remained influential for a long time, Hitler views the Church as an object worthy of observation, even a role model of sorts. It is of interest to him in so far as some of its recipes for success might be effective under the conditions of a modern – Hitler conceives this as a scientifically and technologically advanced – society. Hitler is concerned with the manner in which the Church mobilizes and organizes its Weltanschauung, especially under the conditions of modern competition. He is interested in the Church as a political organization that offers one Weltanschauung in the competitive environment of a pluralist market.

Hitler's critique

The 'slow fading' of the Church: Hitler's scientism

Of course, Hitler's analysis of the Church by no means equates to agreement with its teachings. Although Hitler describes himself as 'pious' and probably called a specific form of religiosity his own, he considers most of the concrete contents of Christian preaching to be refuted by research in the natural sciences. This is why Hitler is convinced that the popularization of scientific insights will conclusively undermine the Church's credibility. 'He who lives naturally [. . .] will inadvertently come into opposition to the Church. This will cause the Church to collapse. Science will reign victorious.' said Hitler in a conversation at the Führer headquarters on 14 October 1941.[22]

This is why it wasn't

right, now to rush into battle with the Church. The best thing to do is to let Christianity slowly fade away; a slow death is also somehow reconciling: the Christian dogma is shattered by science. Already the Church has to make more and more concessions. Thousands of things are gradually becoming spurious. The only thing missing is proof of the fact that in nature, the inorganic and the organic converge without limits! Once knowledge of the universe spreads, once the majority of people realize that stars are not illuminants but worlds, maybe populated worlds such as ours, then Christian teachings will be lead completely ad absurdum.[23]

To Hitler, the 'entire Catholic faith' then, is 'an incredibly clever blend of hypocrisy and enterprise that exploits the human propensity of clinging to established practice.' Even an 'educated clergyman', says Hitler, 'could not possibly believe the nonsense concocted by the Church'.[24] According to a comment made at the Führer headquarters on 13 December 1941, Christianity is 'the maddest thing any delusional human mind has ever produced.' Primarily, and Hitler emphasises this especially, because to him it 'makes a mockery of all things divine'.[25]

And yet Hitler's general scientism, his faith in science, is by no means uninterrupted and it is utterly unaware of its own limitations. To him, science is 'nothing more than a ladder that one climbs: with every rung one can see a little bit further, but even science can not see to the end of all things.'[26] Hitler also doubts that scientific progress and individual happiness are immediately related.

Do scientific insights make men happier? I do not know. But: People are happy with all kinds of different beliefs! Alright, so one also has to be tolerant about this! It is foolish to make man believe he was a conductor in the way that obtrusive liberal science has done in the previous century[27].

But science, says Hitler, 'strives to see things as they are within the constraints of its own understanding. It does not knowingly misrepresent.' Christianity, however, lies. This is why, due to its truth claim, it 'has come into conflict with itself'.

Incidentally, it is also at this point that Hitler poses the question of whether 'deism might not be abolished in general' as Christianity evaporates in modern scientific critique. His answer: 'That wouldn't be good! For the broad mass of people the term "deity" is merely substantiation. This substantiation is wonderful. Why should we destroy the collective term for the unfathomable?' Christianity, though, had 'now indeed', argues Hitler, 'lifted folly to new heights. This is why its constructs will break down entirely one day. Knowledge has already captured all humanity. The more Christianity clings to dogma, the quicker it will fade away.'[29]

Since 'all upheavals are bad' to Hitler, he thinks 'it best if we let the institution of the Church be overcome slowly by spiritual enlightenment making it
painless, giving it a certain clemency. Nunneries could be the very last thing!'[30]
In any case, Hitler sees 'the dawn of a new era, that of the downfall' of the
Church as having arrived:

> It will take a few more centuries, then evolution will achieve what revolution
> hasn't. Every scholar who discovers something new hews away a piece of its
> foundation. It is a shame to live at a time when you cannot yet know what the
> new world will look like,[31]

says Hitler on 11 November 1941.

> The time in which we live sees the appearance of the collapse of matter. It
> may take another one or two hundred years. I am sorry that, like Moses, I
> can see the Promised Land only from afar. We are growing into a sunny,
> truly tolerant Weltanschauung: Man should be in a position to develop the
> skills God granted him. We must only prevent a new and even greater lie
> from developing: the Judeo-Bolshevist world must collapse.[32]

The irreconcilable gulf between words and deeds in
Universalist concepts

Hitler, however, does not only distance himself from the Christian Church
by denouncing its beliefs as irreconcilable with modern science, hence pre-
dicting their imminent loss of influence in large parts of the population.
Significantly, he also accuses the Church of defining itself through words
rather than through deeds with the result that it has lost its credibility. In
Hitler's words, it had become a 'Christianity of Words', no longer one 'of
Deeds'.

This, then, is precisely what Hitler lays claim to for National Socialism: it
is a movement of deeds. In the beginning, Hitler even claims that National
Socialism is the true 'Christianity of Deeds':

> Those who want to keep our Christianity, which, alas, today is merely a
> Christianity of appearances rather than one of deeds, have to confront those
> who rob us of our Christianity. [. . .] Recovery must grow from within us.
> We may be small, but a man once stood up in Galilee and today his teach-
> ings dominate the whole world. I cannot imagine Christ but blond and blue-
> eyed. The devil I can only imagine with the Jewish grimace,[33]

said Hitler at a NSDAP rally in Rosenheim in 1921.

As late as 1937 Hitler employs the cliché image of a child collecting for the *Winterhilfswerk* to play off the true Christianity of (National Socialist) Deeds against the insincere lip service paid by the Church:

> When I see, as I so often do, poorly clad girls collecting with such infinite patience in order to care for those who are suffering from the cold while they themselves are shivering with cold, then I have the feeling that they are all apostles of a Christianity – and in truth of a Christianity which can say with greater right than any other: This is the Christianity of an honest confession, for behind it stand not words but deeds.[34]

Hitler adheres to this line of argument until his death. It can still be found in the 'Political Testament' of 21 February 1945. This once more formulates the concept of a 'National Socialism of Deeds' and significantly develops this idea based on the National Socialist anti-universalism. For it is precisely the inability to act, the falling short of its own demands, the getting stuck in mere 'words' that are immediate results of erroneous 'western' universalism.

To Hitler's mind, universalist concepts can never be the foundation of energetic action. While these aspire to 'the happiness of mankind in the abstract' and thus chase 'the chimera of a formula applicable all the world over,' National Socialism knows 'only [. . .] the German race' and his only interest was in 'the wellbeing of the German man.' Thus 'two families' faced each other of 'wholly irreconcilable outlook in the world'. 'On the one hand, there are the Jews and all those who march in step with them. On the other, there are those who adopt a realistic attitude towards world affairs.'[35] 'The universalists, the idealists , the Utopians,' however, says Hitler,

> all aim too high. They give promise of an unattainable paradise, and by doing so they deceive mankind. Whatever label they wear, whether they call themselves Christians, Communists, humanitarians, whether they are merely sincere but stupid or wire-pullers and cynics, they are all makers of slaves. I myself have always kept my eye fixed on a paradise which, in the nature of things, lies well within our reach. I mean an improvement of the lot of the German people.[36]

'Universalists, idealists, and utopians' – these are the key enemies Hitler identifies in his 'Political Testament' of February 1945. Hitler was firm in his opinion that only an anti-universalist Weltanschauung could be politically workable. For Hitler, both ethical universalism ('All men have equal dignity') and communal religious universalism ('Christianity is objectively true and must therefore hold sway everywhere') are barriers to political action. Ethical universalism 'is aimed into the void' of an earthly paradise for everyone and is hence only something for 'fools' and 'fraudsters'. Communal religious universalism, on the other hand, is simply refuted by facts.

Hitler's ideological ties with the racially legitimized ideology of the *Volksgemeinschaft* are so strong here that even when faced with his own total defeat at the hands of western democracies and the communist Soviet Union he still declares universalist concepts incapable of action. If 'universalists, idealists and utopians' can ultimately only promise the unattainable, Hitler argues, they must necessarily get stuck in the chasm between 'words' and real deeds since their actions fall short of their own words; and not only occasionally, but as a rule. The more so, as Hitler can well see, as that universalist concepts ultimately can only occupy partial social strata, so themselves repudiating and subverting their own universalist claims in the limitations of their social existence. Hitler was very aware of the concrete particularities of religious and/or philosophical claims to validity. He constantly accuses Christianity of making a general and universalist claim, so pronouncing on all men and for all men, but still only ever achieving this through historically and geographically limited particularity. So, for example, during a table talk on 27 February 1942:

> Why does God not make it possible for all men to come to the right idea? From a horizontal perspective, everybody with an education today knows that not even 10 percent of humanity subscribe to Catholicism's idea of God. People created by the same Providence have thousands of different faiths simultaneously. But today we see things vertically as well: we know that this Christianity encompasses only a very brief epoch of humanity.[37]

In the aforementioned 'Political Testament' Hitler then scornfully diagnoses that 'the sum total of the successes of this magnificent Christian religion, the guardian of Supreme Truth' only amounts to 'isolated islets of Christians, Christians in name, that is, rather than by conviction'.[38]

For Hitler, the regionally limited importance and the associated social encapsulation of the denominations, especially in Germany, stand in obvious opposition to what to him is the only possible foundation for action, both politically and 'scientifically': the racially united *Volksgemeinschaft*. 'God did not create our Volk that it be torn apart by priests,' said Hitler in a speech made to Gauleiters at the inauguration of the Ordensburg Sonthofen on 23 November 1937. 'This is why it is necessary to ensure its unity by a system of leadership. That is the task of the NSDAP. It is to comprise that order which, beyond the limits of time and man, is to guarantee the stability of the German development of opinion and hence of the political leadership.'.[39] Hitler continued: 'Today a new state is being established, the unique feature of which is that it sees its foundation not in Christianity and not in a concept of state; rather, it places its primary emphasis on the self-contained Volksgemeinschaft. Hence it is significant that the "German Empire of the German Nation" now puts this supremely capable concept of the future into practice, merciless against all adversaries, against all religious fragmentation, against all fragmentation into parties.'[40]

This battle against the 'denominational fragmentation' of Germany is not only tactically motivated. It follows directly from his racist view of the inexorable struggle between the races, and the idea that the German people, as part of the Aryan race, are the chosen ones. On the basis of the 'word'-'deed'-dichotomy analyzed above, Hitler also demands that his followers reinterpret their denominational affiliation in terms of racist categories for action. 'Everybody who has the right kind of feeling for his country,'* says Hitler,

> is solemnly bound, each within his own denomination, to see to it *that he is not constantly talking about the Will of God merely from the lips but that in actual fact he fulfils the Will of God and does not allow God's handiwork to be debased.*[41]

In *Mein Kampf*, Hitler had already seen 'worse enemies of my country than the international communists' in 'those men who seek to-day to embroil the patriotic movement in religious quarrels.'**[42] 'For it is in the interests of the Jews today,' Hitler continues, 'that the energies of the patriotic movement should be squandered in a religious conflict, because it is beginning to be dangerous for the Jews.'[43]

A résumé

The claim to totality, the collation of the diffuse into dogmas and standards, as well the wisdom garnered from 2000 years of organization, this summarizes what Hitler analyzes and absolutely admires about the Christian Church. All this is of a formal nature. With regard to content, Hitler's critique is aimed at the material preachings of the Church, which to his mind have been definitively discredited by modern (natural) science.

But Hitler's critique exceeds this trivial scientistic line of argument. The irreconcilability of the principles of Christian preaching with 'modern consciousness' not only has repercussions for their plausibility in the consciousness of individuals, but, according to Hitler, it also affects the possibilities of configuring Church as a social organism capable of action. He continues to detect universalist concepts underpinning Christian teachings. These, however, remain incapable of action for Hitler, who believes they are directed into

---

* This is a problematic translation of 'Gerade der völkisch Eingestellte' (630) as it attempts to render *völkisch* as related purely to country thus neglecting the strong racial overtones.
** Again, the translation is problematic: 'völkische Bewegung' is couched as 'patriotic movement' and 'Volk' has become country.

the void due to their inability to concretize without at the same time implicitly betraying their own universalist claim. He argues that Christian concepts are permanently pulverised between the Church's demand, 'the word' aimed at the whole, and its own actions, which then fall short of its demand of 'deeds'.

The Church, perforce, escaped into the intellectualism of the word on the one hand and a kind of configuration that was merely particular on the other; the latter having to conceal its own confessional and regional particularity. It is not difficult to draw parallels between these two variants and the threats to the two major Christian denominations.

Under the conditions of modernity, though, the creation of a social organization capable of political action is impossible for Hitler on the basis of such an implicitly contradictory foundation. Hitler's solution is just as simple as it is effective: The categorical dismissal of universalism solves the characteristically modern problem of the chasm between the claim to universality and merely regional plausibility. 'Word' and 'deed', the claim to universality and historically contingent realities, thus remain communicable.

According to Hitler, a powerful political institution based on a *Weltanschauung* can only be created under the conditions of pluralist modernity once universalism has been discarded. He himself exemplifies this with the ideologeme of the *Volksgemeinschaft*. For it is only after such a cut has been made that the chasm between ambition and reality, which destroys all plausibility, can be overcome in the individual's consciousness; if, that is, the 'word' – or the propagation of the Weltanschauung – is conferred with an identifiable and realistic social base. Where this includes, as it does with Hitler, recourse to the social Darwinist interpretation of biological theories and thus is furnished with a 'scientific' legitimization,[44] the connection to modernity is secured.

Hitler sees the Church's outstanding achievement in the potential its teachings have to totalize, standardize and concretize. Its existentially threatening weakness, however, he sees both in its antiquated ecclesiastical 'Weltanschauung' and the aforementioned gulf between 'word' and 'deed'. The latter is seen to be evidenced by the Christian claim to universality and the recognizably regional reach of this claim that is inevitable in modernity. Put together, these weaknesses inexorably destroy the foundations of the impressive ruling techniques and concretizing achievements of the ecclesiastical institutions, according to Hitler. He is convinced that an institution based on a Weltanschauung can only be plausible and capable of action if it connects to the knowledge of the present as well as avoiding being pulverized between its own claims of universality and a discernible regionalizm necessitated by modernity. Hitler sees both of these as given in his political project of a racially united *Volksgemeinschaft*.

Institutionally speaking, however, Hitler does not want another Church. He wants the individual, the public and religion to come together in a new configuration based on politics:

This is why I envision the future as follows: Initially everybody has their private faith; superstition will also always play a part. The party does not run the risk of becoming a rival organization to the Church. We have to enforce that the Church no longer interferes with the State. The education of youth ensures that everybody knows what is right in terms of preserving the State. [. . .] We will ensure that the Church no longer proclaims any teachings that contradict our own teachings. We will continue to enforce our National Socialist teachings and the youth will hence forward only hear the truth.[45]

Notes

1 Cf.: Gruber, *Katholische Kirche*; Siegele-Wenschkewitz, *Nationalsozialismus und Kirche*; Kretschmar, *Dokumente zur Kirchenpolitik*; Conway, *The Nazi Persecution of the Churches*.

2 Hitler, *Sämtliche Aufzeichnungen*, 636 (NSDAP bulletin of 26 April 1922).

3 Hitler, *Mein Kampf*, 199.

4 Ibid., 254.

5 Hitler, *Reden, Schriften und Anordnungen III*. I quote from the original manuscript at hand (Staatsarchiv Nürnberg, NS Mischbestand (Sam. Streicher, Nr. 116)), 26.

6 Hitler, *Mein Kampf*, 254.

7 Ibid.

8 Picker, *Hitlers Tischgespräche*, 247 (4 April 1942).

9 Hitler, *Mein Kampf*, 214–15.

10 Ibid., 152.

11 Ibid.

12 Ibid.

13 Cf.: Arnold, *Modernismus*; Weiß, *Modernismus*; Bucher, *Kirchenbildung*, 39–78.

14 Hitler, *Mein Kampf*, 257.

15 Ibid.

16 Ibid., 125 [emphasis in Murphy's translation].

17 Hitler also very generously discusses the NSDAP party programme. It will only very limitedly become the basis for the National Socialist State. Simultaneously, it is publicly declared to be unchangeable. Cf.: Jäckel, *Hitlers Weltanschauung*, 80–5; Kershaw, *Hitler I*, 189.

18 For Hitler's thoughts on this cf.: Zitelmann, *Hitler*, 364–75.

19 Picker, *Hitlers Tischgespräche*, 235 (31 March 1942).

20 Ibid., 236 (31 March 1942).

21 Hitler, *Mein Kampf*, 242.

22 Hitler, *Monologe*, 85 (14 October 1941).

23 Ibid., 83.

24 Picker, *Hitlers Tischgespräche*, 267 (9 November 1941).

25 Hitler, *Monologe*, 150 (13 December 1941).

[26] Ibid., 103 (24 October 1941).

[27] Ibid., 103, 105.

[28] Ibid., 85 (14 October 1941).

[29] Ibid., 84.

[30] Ibid., 135 (11 November 1941).

[31] Ibid., 136 (11 November 1941).

[32] Ibid., 303 (27 February 1942).

[33] Hitler, *Sämtliche Aufzeichnungen*, 367 (21 April 1921).

[34] Hitler, *The Speeches of Adolf Hitler*, Vol I, 393 (Speech given on 5 October 1937).

[35] Trevor-Roper/François-Poncet, *The Testament of Adolf Hitler*, 82–3 (21 February 1945).

[36] Ibid., 83.

[37] Hitler, *Monologe*, 301 (14 October 1941).

[38] Trevor-Roper/François-Poncet, *The Testament of Adolf Hitler*, 45 (7 February 1945).

[39] Domarus, *Hitler*, 981 (Speech given 23 November 1937 to *Kreis-* and *Gauleiters*).

[40] Ibid., 979f.

[41] Hitler, *Mein Kampf*, 310. Also compare the earlier comment: 'Those who do not want our Christianity – which today, unfortunately, is merely a Christianity of appearances rather than one of actions – to be lost, must fight the man who would rob us of our Christianity.' (Hitler, *Sämtliche Aufzeichnungen*, 367 (Speech held at a NSDAP assembly in Rosenheim 21 April 1921)) [Emphasis RB].

[42] Hitler, *Mein Kampf*, 311.

[43] Ibid.

[44] Cf. Poliakov, *Der arische Mythos*; Miles, *Racism*; Weingart/Kroll/Bayertz, *Rasse, Blut und Gene*. Von Barkhaus' study, 'Rasse' impressively demonstrates that it was precisely modern scientific discourse that created the notion of race: 'The notion of race is a product of the anthropological discourse at the end of the eighteenth century and as such it is a significant example for a scientific construction of reality that penetrates the experiential realm of lived experience and determines every-day perceptions.' After the loss of authority of the key early modern pattern of interpretation, religion [. . .] 'race' turns into an important modern pattern for the interpretation of social reality – far beyond its scientific significance.' (267).

[45] Hitler, *Monologe*, 85.

Chapter 3

Hitler and the Theology of the '*Völkisch* Movement'

The religiosity of the '*völkisch* Movement'

Hitler sees Christians, democrats, socialists – just about all 'universalists' as hopelessly enmeshed in the chasm between their universalist claims and the always limited reach of these demands in reality; especially since this limited reach has become highly visible in modernity. Hitler's way out of this dilemma is simple: he dismisses universalism as an ethical concept that sees all men as equal. Instead, he focuses on a *völkisch* unity, the German people, or (in all likelihood purposefully) vaguely expanded, the Aryan race. According to Hitler, ultimately only the Aryan race deserves what universalism terms human dignity.

This 'Aryan race', and within it centrally the 'German people', is accorded nothing less than the claim to universal world dominion. This is a decidedly anti-universalist universalism. It is typical of the '*völkisch* Movement' that began long before Hitler's time but that influenced him during his Vienna years.[1] Initially, Hitler sees himself primarily as its 'drummer [boy]'[2] before understanding himself to be its executor and its fulfilment.

The '*völkisch* Movement', however, provides its own religious tradition and practice,[3] that is, it has its own theology. Doubtlessly, Hitler also encounters this theology, particularly during his time in Vienna.[4] Contrary to many beliefs still widespread today, a look at Hitler's writings, speeches and notes shows: Hitler does *not* fall back on this obvious and readily available possibility of tying his own political project into an existing religiosity. In fact, he explicitly, consistently, and unequivocally rejects *völkisch* religiosity from the beginning. He deems it unsuitable for his National Socialist social project.

The '*völkisch* religion' had developed during the crises of modernity. On the one hand, it was a niche phenomenon that comprised small, meditative circles that had often also fallen out internally. On the other hand, it was not unattractive beyond these circles, either. For example *Ostara*, the magazine published by 'Baron Johannes Lancz de Liebenfels' (really: Joseph Adolf Lanz), whose ingredients were racism, aggressive misogyny, and occultism, was definitely also read in 'better circles', not to mention by authors such as Julius Langbehn, Wagner's son-in-law Houston Stewart Chamberlain or Paul de Lagarde. All of these men, albeit religiously grounded racists, were men of prestige and high esteem.

This anti-Christian, Germanizing religiosity, rejected by the Church as 'neo-pagan', was racist, mostly anti-feminist, and of a 'boys' club' attitude. It was anti-Jewish and anti-ecclesiastical. Occasionally, it radically reinterpreted Christianity. Occasionally it strictly opposed it. It practically always had roman-ticizing and archaizing tendencies. It invoked 'scientific' insights that were largely invented and above all else were anti-universalist. This religiosity con-veyed superiority, scientificity, the liberation from Christian morality, and the rediscovery of buried matter, matter that had been overlaid with 'un-German' layers by Judaism and Christianity. And yet this religiosity was purely the con-coction of its 'founders'.

Surely the most radical of these religiously grounded race fanatics, as evi-denced in the tone and content of his obscene *Ostara* magazine, was Lanz von Liebenfels. But the view that race breeding [*Rassenzucht*] and blood purity [*Blutreinhaltung*] were necessary or at least desirable was widely spread in bourgeois circles around 1900. The existence of noble Aryans and inferior mixed races [*Mischrasse*] was taken for granted. Lanz' 'Order of New Templars' included quite wealthy and respectable men; after all, Lanz was able to acquire the Werfenstein ruin on the banks of the Danube with their donations.

National Socialism included followers and propagandists of '*völkisch* religios-ity', for example Heinrich Himmler and *Reichsbauernführer* Darré. Hitler, too, was certainly influenced by it and agrees both with its racist principles and with its rejection of Christianity. He was not, however, a follower of '*völkisch* religiosity'.

Hitler's rejection of '*völkisch* religiosity'

Early days and *Mein Kampf*

The reason for this was just as simple as it was compelling: It was impossible to found a state on it, let alone the modern state envisioned by Hitler. From the beginning, Hitler explicitly, consistently, and unequivocally dismisses '*völkisch* religiosity'. He deems it unsuitable for his National Socialist social project.

Hitler is doubtlessly familiar with the racist agents of *völkisch* religiosity and is also directly influenced by them, for example through Dietrich Eckart[5] to whom he dedicates *Mein Kampf*. In addition, distinguishing his project from '*völkisch* religiosity' demanded enormous and highly risky theoretical, but even more so politically tactical efforts on Hitler's part. This was especially the case in the 1920s, a time when his movement was anything but consolidated. At times during this process, when his party was still weak and insignificant, Hitler disassociated himself from previous comrades-in-arms from the *völkisch*

Movement, so for example Artur Dinter[6] or the increasingly religiously fac-
tious World War General Ludendorf.[7] Hitler's tactics towards achieving political legality, which he pursued after his release from Landsberg Prison (20
December 1924), were certainly behind this disassociation. The aim of this tac-
tic was to 'appear simultaneously as revolutionary and as defender of existing
conditions, radical and moderate at once. He must both threaten the system
and play the part of its preserver,'[8] as Joachim Fest aptly analyzes.

In the mid-1920s Hitler is doubtlessly also, but not exclusively, concerned
with reassuring the consciences of potential Christian followers and thus
ensuring his connectibility with German Christian culture.[9] Within his party,
Hitler determinedly disempowered the propagandists of Germanic religiosity
in order to then functionalise these men in small dosages against the existent
official Church [*Großkirche*].[10] One example of this is Rosenberg. With respect
to questions of religion, Hitler was now no longer willing 'to tolerate offences
from his followers, even though in other respects he made allowances for political slips and even criminal weaknesses without much ado.'[11]

However, it was precisely not purely for tactical or strategic reasons in the
face of state authorities and specifically the Church that Hitler parted from the
inner-party proponents of '*völkisch* religiosity'. He realized that his racist world
redemption project simply stood no chance of political success with such a religious position. Hitler also defines the theological principles of his project himself. In terms of its intentions, especially its racism and its anti-universalism,
it is similar to '*völkisch* religiosity'; but it is also clearly distinct from it. Hitler
particularly lacks any inclinations towards obscurantism, *völkisch* romanticiza-
tion and even Germanizing polytheism. Since *Mein Kampf* at the latest, Hitler
has nothing but 'biting scorn'[12] for these.

Hitler's political project, as he himself clearly sees, is not feasible on the
basis of a neo-pagan religiosity that is hostile towards modernity. Religion is
doubtlessly a crucial element of Hitler's project, but it is precisely not the religiosity of those circles that make an apparently ingenious religious offering to
National Socialism. Hitler develops his own dispositif of religion.

In the long run, Hitler did reap political benefits from distancing himself from
von Rosenberg and other 'neo-pagan' propagandists. As Ian Kershaw notes, even
during the so-called Church struggle during the early years of Hitler's rule,

> church-going Christians, so often encouraged by their 'opinion leaders' in
> the Church hierarchies, were frequently able to exclude Hitler from their
> condemnation of the atheist Nazi ideology and the anti-Christian Party rad-
> icals, continuing to see in him the last hope of protecting Christianity from
> godless Bolshevism.[13]

For good reason Hitler saw himself forced to exclude genuine religiosity from
his movement. Above all: the theology of '*völkisch* religiosity' did not connect

to modernity in the way that Hitler desired andconceived it. His own project, in any case, he saw as a specific variant of modernity, not as a return to pre-modern or even pre-Christian mythologies. So he developed his own theo-logical concept: an independent 'theology of anti-pluralist modernity'.

In 1968 Friedrich Heer already notes that Hitler 'emphatically [distances] himself from all movements related to *völkisch*, neo-pagan, or Germanic ideas'. He continues by arguing that to a large extent *Mein Kampf* gives the impression that 'it was written against these circles in particular.'[14] So Hitler's programmatic magnum opus is also unequivocal in its stance towards '*völkisch* religiosity':

> The impression which I often get, especially of those so-called religious reformers who whose creed is grounded on ancient Germanic customs, is that they are the missionaries and protégés of those forces which do not wish to see a national revival taking place in Germany. All their activities tend to turn the attention of the people away from the necessity of fighting together in a common enemy, namely the Jew. Moreover, that kind of preaching induces the people to use up their energies, not in fighting for the common cause, but in absurd and ruinous religious controversies within their own ranks. [. . .] I need not call attention to the absolute lack of worldly wisdom, and especially the failure to understand the soul of the nation, which is dis-played by these Messianic Precursors of the Twentieth Century.[15]

Elsewhere in his programmatic writing, Hitler argues that,

> [n]ot less dangerous are those that run about as semi-folkists formulating fantastic schemes which are mostly based on nothing else than a fixed idea which in itself might be right but which, because it is an isolated notion, is of no use whatsoever for the formation of a great homogeneous fighting asso-ciation and could by no means serve as the basis of its organization. Those people [. . .] are often more dangerous than the outspoken enemies of the *völkisch* idea. At best they are sterile theorists but more frequently they are mischievous agitators of the public mind. They believe that they can mask their intellectual vanity, the futility of their efforts, and their lack of stability, by sporting flowing beards and indulging in ancient German gestures.[16]

Hitler's rejection of '*völkisch* religiosity' is as unambiguous as it is consistent. As early as 1922, and thus prior to *Mein Kampf*, Hitler had already written the following in the *Völkischer Beobachter*:

> *A multitude of dreamers appeared and drew forth all the old stuff that German history seemed to contain. They seemed to forget that we are not living in the year 600 or 700, but in 1920, forgetting that the needs and demands of our current times are different from those one and a half thousand years ago.* The *völkisch* Movement turned into

a hotbed for well-meaning fools, all the more dangerous for it. Rapturous jurists rummaged around in medieval legal codes, devoured the *Sachsen-* and *Schwabenspiegel* and thought they could move an entire people backwards by a thousand years without problem. They did not realize, caught up in their own unwordliness, that it could never be about the rebirth of antediluvian forms, but that a new Germanic body of law which was perfectly aligned with the economic conditions of our time and corresponded deeply with the feeling of our blood, the instinct of our race, had to be created.[17]

After 1933

Hitler consistently emphasises the irreconcilability between neo-pagan '*völkisch* religiosity' and the National Socialist project. His argument is based above all on the lack of connectibility between this religious form and modernity, due to the former's untenability in the face of modern reason. '*National Socialism* is a cool-headed *doctrine of realities*; it mirrors clearly scientific knowledge and its expression in thought,' exclaims Hitler in his 'Proclamation by the Führer at the party rally' on 6 September 1938. 'Since we have won the heart of our people for this doctrine "we do not wish to fill their minds with mysticism which lies outside of that doctrine's goal and purpose."' And he continues:

> We will *not allow* mystically-minded occult folk with a passion for exploring the secrets of the world beyond to steal into our Movement. Such folk are not National Socialists, but something else – in any case something which has nothing to do with us.[18]

Ultimately, Hitler's rejection of '*völkisch* religiosity' goes as far as publicly denying that National Socialism encompasses anything akin to the cultic or the ecclesiastic; even though this disavowal contradicts all evidence provided by the manner of its actual orchestration. Evidently, the public distinction of the National Socialist project from traditional institutions that govern religion as well as from the neo-pagan currents within the '*völkisch* Movement' itself is extraordinarily important to Hitler.

> *National Socialism is not a cult-movement – a movement for worship; it is exclusively a 'volkic' political doctrine based upon racial principles. In its purpose there is no mystic cult, only the care and leadership of a people defined by a common blood-relationship. Therefore we have no rooms for worship, but only halls for the people – no open spaces for worship, but spaces for assemblies and parades. We have no religious retreats, but arenas for sports and playing-fields, and the characteristic feature of our places of assembly is not the mystical gloom of a cathedral, but the brightness and light of a room or hall which combines beauty with fitness for its purpose.[19]*

Certainly, as will be shown, this distancing is the result of the need to distinguish an alternative project that integrates religion and is laden with theology, it is not, however, a result of its own lack of religion or theology. In smaller circles Hitler then also talks differently. The following entry can be found in Goebbel's diary for 7 August 1933: '*Gautag.* [. . .] Stirring moment. Hitler speaks for 3 hours. About the more distant future. Otherwise, founding [uncertain decipherment, R.B.] Harsh against the Church. We will ourselves become a Church.'[20] Goebbels is referring to a speech for the NSDAP *Reichs-* and *Gauleiter* given by Hitler on 5 March. The text of this speech, though, remains unknown.[21] In the speech just cited, given at the party rally of 1938, Hitler's course of action with respect to the politics of terminology becomes evident. Hitler massively distances National Socialism from cult and Church in the same breath as he attempts to assign new, National Socialist meanings to classic terms from cult and Church.

Hitler significantly figures the difference in meaning between these terms as used in Christianity but also as used in 'neo-pagan' religiosity and as used by him via the Enlightenment metaphor of light. It has to be noted, though: Hitler is not concerned with opposing and distinguishing a generally unenlightened, obscurantist religion to and from Enlightenment, science and modernity. Instead, he is concerned with the distinction between enlightened and unenlightened religion, with action that takes place not 'in the secretive glow of the twilight of a place of ritual worship, but before the open countenance of the Lord' as Hitler ultimately posits.

The quotation in full:

> Our programme is not headed by mysterious ideas, but by *clear realization* and thus *openly declared beliefs.* By centring this realization and these beliefs on the preservation and thus the sustainment of a being created by God, we are thus serving to preserver divine creating and thus the fulfilment of divine will. And we are doing this not in the secretive glow of the twilight of a place of ritual worship, but before the open countenance of the Lord. There have been eras, when semi-darkness was the pre-condition for the effectiveness of certain teachings. Today is the era when *light* is the basic condition for the success of our actions. [. . .] Our cult states exclusively: Care for the *natural* and thus also that which is *desired by God.* Our humility is the unconditional obeisance to and respect for the divine laws of being as they are revealed to us humans. Our prayer reads: Bravely fulfil the duties arising from this. We are not, however, responsible for ritual – that is the responsibility of the *Church*! Should anybody, though, think that these our duties might not be enough for or no relate to him, then he must prove that God intends to make us of him, to do a better job.[22]

To Hitler, then, the ultimate and only convincing evidence of the legitimacy of his political project is the proof of its divine legitimation!

Hitler's religious political project accepts modernity with its cognitive structures based on science – in the way that he comprehends them. Hitler demands a kind of religiosity that is reconcilable with the scientific culture of modernity. In his view, neither Christianity nor '*völkisch* religiosity' accomplish this. This means they are outdated and only of interest from an antiquarian perspective. It nearly seems as though Hitler were only interested in instrumentalizing religion, as though he reduces it to its social and political function.

'Religion', he meditates in a select circle on 14 October 1941,

> was primarily the support for the construction of a human society. It was a means, not an end in itself! [. . .] The sanitary content of nearly all religions was an incredible help for the construction of a state. [. . .] The whole thing a path towards building human social organisms without which peoples would never have obtained the forms they take today.[23]

But even at this point a second level, one that transcends the pure functionalization of religion, becomes visible. To Hitler, religion is more than fiction, more than a useful means to integrate society and build a state. It is 'reverence of the incognizable'. This 'incognizable', then, is addressed and comprehended in different ways by men, dependent on their individual state of enlightenment, thinks Hitler. The ideal way of arriving at enlightenment is what Hitler calls 'internalization'. This

> can take place by way of a conscious submersion into nature or through the study of history. However, only a minority has these abilities and this is he who is gripped by reverence in the face of the incognisable and finds metaphysical fulfilment in it.[24]

Beneath this path of enlightenment runs the path of simplicity. For 'the little man also desires the metaphysical, but it can only be fulfilled for him by an internalisation that sets itself apart from this path. [. . .] Ordinary people affectively cling to celestial aid.'[25] After all, for the 'broad masses the term deity is just a substantiation'.[26]

While the path of the 'little man' may be deficient, it is neither one of deceit, nor fraud, nor illusion. Hitler's 'enlightenment' of religion is not concerned with exposing every religion, but with the analysis of – in his view – imperfect religion. But to Hitler it is imperfect in its Christian manifestation, to his mind the 'height of foolishness' since its 'construction' would 'shatter completely'[27] in the face of contemporary science, as he puts it during said table talk on 14 October 1941.

To his mind perhaps even more foolish, though, is '*völkisch* religion'. To Hitler, as expressed in a table talk in 1941, it seemed 'indescribably foolish, to revive a cult of Wotan. Our ancient mythology of gods was outdated, was no longer viable, when Christianity appeared. Only that which is ready to perish ever disappears!'[28] This is why it would be wrong altogether to want to replace the Church with a '*völkisch* religiosity'. Whoever wished to do this, in any case, should do it beyond the realm of politics for this was precisely where '*völkisch* religion' could be of no good whatsoever.

'Do you feel that Providence has called you to proclaim the Truth to the world?' Hitler asks the propagandists of a neo-pagan religion in *Mein Kampf*:

> If so, then go and do it. But you ought to have the courage to do it directly and not use some political party as your mouthpiece; [. . .] In the place of something that now exists and is bad put something else that is better and will last into the future. If you lack the requisite courage or if you your-self do not know clearly what your better substitute ought to be, leave the whole thing alone. But, whatever happens, do not try to reach the goal by the roundabout way of a political party if you are not brave enough to fight with your visor lifted.[29]

Criticizing Rosenberg

Hitler's verdict also strikes out at Rosenberg's *The Myth of the Twentieth Century*, which to the public was basically the ideologically foundational party-political work. Hitler is reported to have said the following during one of his table talks on 11 April 1942: 'At dinner, the boss emphasizes that Rosenberg's *Myth* could not be considered a party-political work.'[30] He continues by saying that

> he, the boss, had expressly rejected conferring party-pontifical status to the book at the time, since even its title was crooked. For one could not say that one wanted to pit the spiritual understandings of the nineteenth century against the myth, that is, something mystical, of the twentieth century. Instead, as a National Socialist, one had to say that one pitted twentieth century faith and knowledge against the myth of the nineteenth century.[31]

It is noteworthy that Hitler is not pitting knowledge, but *faith* and knowledge against myth.

Historically interesting, by the way, is the continuation of Hitler's explanation at this point: 'It is remarkable,' the reporter of Hitler's table talk continues,

> that the main readership of Rosenberg's work was not to be found amongst old party comrades. In fact, there were great difficulties initially in even sell-ing the first edition. Not until the work was mentioned in a pastoral letter were the first 10.000 copies successfully sold off. The second edition was only made possible because the Munich Cardinal Faulhaber so stupidly quoted

from *Myth* at a Bishops' Conference. Once the book had then been black-listed due to the accusation of party heresy, the demand for the book rose further. And when the Catholic Church then published all its pamphlets of responses against Rosenberg's thoughts, the print run climbed to 170,000 and 200,000 respectively. He, the boss, was always pleased, when he was forced to discover that only our enemies really knew their way around the book. Similarly to many *Gauleiter*, he also had only read a small part of it, because it was also too incomprehensibly written.[32]

Conclusion

Hitler's examination of the *Christian Church* was above all a formal analysis of its constitutional principles. Simultaneously, he massively critiques the contents of Christian preaching. On the whole, he deems the Church refuted by the Enlightenment and by science and sees it as an institutionalization of religion incompatible with modernity. Put slightly more bluntly: Through his examin-ation of the Church Hitler develops the beginnings of his 'Practical Theology', that is, a theology that asks: 'How does Church (as an organization delivering a Weltanschauung) work practically and what can I take away from it?'

According to Hitler, '*völkisch* religiosity', by contrast, does not offer any knowledge of the processes of social constitution or the processes of religious institutionalization comparable to Christianity. This is shown in its effects of atomisation and fragmentation alone. In addition to its scientifically abstruse suppositions, this is why Hitler deems '*völkisch* religiosity' completely unsuit-able as a religious component of the National Socialist project.

His critique of '*völkisch* religiosity' is thus one of a religion adverse to modernity in *all* its components. As much as Hitler, as remains to be shown, shares some of the basic principles of this '*völkisch* theology', for example the racism, the heroism, or the idea of world dominion, he also emphasises that this '*völkisch* religion' is even more abstruse than Christianity when confronted with the scientific reason of modernity. Through a discussion of this '*völkisch* theology' Hitler thus develops something akin to his own 'religious philoso-phy' and reflects on the function and rationality of religion in general.

Religion for Hitler means reverence for the incomprehensible. The com-mon, notion of God pertaining to substantiation, however, is the insufficiently complex version of this 'metaphysical' experience of the incomprehen-sible in history and nature, as he also calls it. This is just as vague as it is, in the first instance, in and of itself undangerous. Hitler's rejection of the '*völkisch* weirdo' and 'occult researchers into the afterlife' is, after all, only too understandable.

It becomes dangerous when those connections are made, which now sug-gest themselves. The connection between vague religiosity as the idea of the incomprehensibility of the world and history in general, racism that understands itself as scientifically proven, and the messianic idea of having been chosen, the latter of which is directed at the person himself with increasing clarity.

And it is precisely these connections that Hitler now makes. This does, however, show that Hitler's theology is heir to revealed religions with its idea of messianic election, the eighteenth century concept of religion, and nine-teenth-century scientism. Hitler becomes a typical agent of the twentieth century by then short-circuiting all of these and consolidating them into a political project.

Notes

[1] Cf.: Hamann, *Hitler's Vienna*, 200–35.

[2] Cf.: Tyrell, *Vom 'Trommler' zum 'Führer'*.

[3] On '*völkisch* religiosity' see: Goodrick-Clarke, *Die okkulten Wurzeln*; Mendle-witsch, *Volk und Heil*; Flasche, *Vom Deutschen Kaiserreich zum Dritten Reich*; Hieronimus, *Zur Religiosität der völkischen Bewegung*; Cancik, 'Neuheiden' und totaler Staat (Lit.); Hieronimus, *Zur Frage nach dem Politischen*. More of a popu-larist perspective: Gugenberger, *Hitlers Visionäre*. For a survey of existing research: Schnurbein/Ulbricht, *Völkische Religion*.

[4] Jörg Lanz von Liebenfels' 'Ariosophie' is worth mentioning here, as is Artur Dinters' 'Geistchristentum' both of which clearly influenced Hitler's early ideo-logical development to a degree. See: Hamann, *Hitler's Vienna*, 200–35. The actual extent of this influence, however, remains undetermined due to the lim-ited source material available. Kershaw (*Hitler I*, 51f.) is much more cautious here. For example, it cannot be said with absolute certainty that Hitler even actually read *Ostara*.

[5] On Eckart: Bärsch, *Politische Religion*, 60–98.

[6] Cf.: Kershaw, *Hitler I*, 264f.

[7] On this see also: Scholder, *Die Kirchen und das Dritte Reich I*, 110–23 ('Hitlers kirchenpolitische Grundentscheidungen 1924–1928'); Bollmus, *Das Amt Rosen-berg*; Zitelmann, *Hitler*, 331–7.

[8] Fest, *Hitler*, 224.

[9] This aspect is particularly drawn out by Scholder, *Die Kirchen und das Dritte Reich I*, 110–23 and it should, without a doubt, be taken into consideration since it demonstrates Hitler's extraordinary strategic far-sightedness. In *Hitler und die katholische Kirche*, Hoser also emphasises that 'after re-entering politics [Hitler] taboos the treatment of religious questions for tactical reasons' (483). Simulta-neously, as Hoser notes, 'the relationship with the Church' had evidently turned into a 'controversial issue' for Hitler and was the 'occasion for obsessive monolo-gising without actually being prepared to discuss' (ibid.). The latter, especially, points to a more than purely tactical interest on Hitler's part.

[10] On the Catholic debate surrounding Rosenberg: Burkard, *Häresie und Mythus*; Baumgärtner, *Weltanschauungskampf*.

11 Hoser, *Hitler und die katholische Kirche*, 483.

12 Fest, *Hitler*, 226.

13 Kershaw, '*Hitler Myth*', 109.

14 Heer, *Der Glaube des Adolf Hitler*, 221.

15 Hitler, *Mein Kampf*, 205f.

16 Ibid., 259.

17 Hitler, *Sämtliche Aufzeichnungen*, 551 (*Völkischer Beobachter*, 25 January 1922).

18 Hitler, *The Speeches of Adolf Hitler*, Vol I, 395f. (Proclamation by the Führer at the party rally on 6 September 1938.)

19 Ibid.

20 Fröhlich, *Die Tagebücher von Joseph Goebbels I*, vol. 2, 455.

21 On this speech and its significance within Hitler's Church policy see: Siegele-Wenschkewitz, *Nationalsozialismus und Kirche*, 127–31.

22 Hitler, *Ausgewählte Reden*, 29f.

23 Hitler, *Monologe*, 83f (14 October 1941).

24 Ibid., 84.

25 Ibid.

26 Ibid., 85.

27 Ibid., 84.

28 Ibid.

29 Ibid., 74.

30 Picker, *Hitlers Tischgespräche*, 269f (11 April 1942).

31 Ibid., 269.

32 Ibid., 269f.

Part II

Structures and Concepts

Chapter 4

'Providence': Hitler's Theology of History

Hitler's theology combines a vague philosophy of religion, where religiosity is understood as an idea of the incomprehensibility of the world and of history, with both a kind of racism that believes itself scientifically proven and a pronounced sense of calling. But how does this work in terms of content? Which categories and terms does Hitler employ?

The 'ex negativo' usage before 1933:
Weimar – 'not chosen by Providence'

Hitler's excessive use of the idea of Providence is surely the most conspicuous and thus also the most well-known. Literally hardly any of Hitler's public speeches after 1933 abstain from using this category from the theology of history, abstain from fitting his own project into a divine course of history. Initially, this reference remains relatively undetermined; it is applied more ex negativo to the Weimar constitutional period and its political agents. Later Hitler will apply this category to himself in a positive sense and spell it out ever more concretely.

The category of Providence was, like many a category in Hitler's theology, cleverly positioned between traditional Christian language usage and general religious vocabulary. Rhetorically, it was very effective from the start, but this particular category was concerned with more than just rhetoric. As early as in a speech to party comrades given in Munich on 30 October 1923 Hitler's critique of democratic politicians culminates in the verdict that 'none of them' were 'chosen by Providence', rather, they were all of them 'products of parliamentary convenience.'[1]

This opposition illustrates Hitler's view that only he, who is legitimized by 'Providence', can justly claim the right to rule as well as to a following. To Hitler, illegitimacy above all means not to have been 'chosen by Providence' – he who is 'not chosen by Providence' is not a legitimate political authority. The reverse is true for Hitler: 'Providence' is the key legitimizing authority for political rule.

As yet, however, Hitler shies away from directly applying the idea of Providence to his National Socialist project let alone to himself.[2] Conceived in categories that seem, in comparison to the idea of Providence, much more reserved and careful albeit already grounded in theology, Hitler sees National Socialism for the time being much more as a 'wonder during a period of decline', as an 'army of millions [. . .] of faithful Germans', that had stepped up to redeem Germany: 'Our movement, that gave a new faith to millions of people, can also give them fulfilment.'[3]

National Socialism as a project of 'Providence': *Mein Kampf*

In *Mein Kampf* this reservation is, still carefully but quite distinctly, abandoned. Hitler ventures to apply the idea of Providence to the National Socialist project with increasing explicitness and in isolated instances he also already applies it to himself. Hitler now 'fervidly thank[s] Providence' which 'sent' him to the 'school' that was the years of suffering in Vienna.[4] With a view to the poor propaganda work during the early days of the movement, Hitler

> was tormented by the thought that if Providence had put the conduct of German propaganda into my hands, instead of into the hands of those incompetent and even criminal ignoramuses and weaklings, the outcome of the struggle might have been different.[5]

As yet, however, the idea of Providence remains above all a category of legit-imization for all those institutions of social rule that can legitimately demand obedience. '[T]he State,' says Hitler, is not

> a compact made between contracting parties, with a certain delimited ter-ritory, for the purpose of serving economic ends. The State is a community of living beings who have kindred physical and spiritual natures, organized for the purpose of assuring the conservation of their own kind and to help towards fulfilling those ends which Providence has assigned to that particu-lar race or racial branch.[6]

Clearly, the idea of Providence here serves the purpose of justifying the State goals of a 'true State'. Consequently, in a 1932 speech given to the Industry Club in Düsseldorf Hitler argues that the Treaty of Versailles is 'not something which has been burdened or imposed upon us by Providence,' it is 'the work of man for which, quite naturally, once again men will have to be held respon-sible, with their merits and with their faults.'[7]

This illustrates that while in *Mein Kampf* the idea of Providence finally turns into a means of justification that in itself no longer requires justification, Hitler uses it only very cautiously and only indirectly applies it to himself. Also, where Hitler does apply the idea of Providence directly to himself it remains oddly lacking in function, appears casually introduced.

Post-1933: 'Heaven and Providence have blessed our efforts'

This changes significantly with National Socialism's victory over the Weimar Democracy. After 1933, Hitler refers to the category of Providence with increased frequency and less mindfulness. In order to justify the abolition of the democratic 'system', he meshes the National Socialist seizure of power and the idea of Providence into the context of a theology of history that is beyond mere 'works of man'. The difficulty and the intermittent hopelessness of the National Socialist struggle are precisely what prove the providential necessity of the victory of the National Socialist project.

This use of the idea of Providence in the offensive can be found as early as his programmatic speech to the Reichstag on 'Potsdam Day' (21 March 1933). 'Potsdam Day' was an important milestone in the staging of Hitler virtually as the 'natural' consequence of German political development. It served to inaugurate Hitler the statesman, his self-proclaimed joining of the ranks of German history.[8] It is particularly through the idea of Providence that Hitler connects to the period preceding his own when he claims that it was 'Providence' that had given Hindenburg 'the privilege of being the patron of the new *Erhebung* [uprising] of our Volk.'[9] Upon Hindenburg's death Hitler confesses to the German people via the radio: 'In the past year and a half, I have thanked Providence again and again that It decreed that the National Socialist Movement, through me, was able to render its pledge of loyalty to this true father of the nation.'[10]

In 1933 Hitler's theology still purports to know that

all human labours are doomed to fail if they are not blessed by the light of Providence. But we do not belong to those who comfortably rely on a here-after. Nothing will be given us for free. Just as, for us, the road from the past fourteen years to the present day has been a road of incessant struggle, a road which often led us near despair, the road to a better future will also be difficult.[11]

Not until after the seizure of power does Hitler dare summon divine succour directly. He ascribes its achievement, its success to this succour: 'As God is my witness: this work has no other aim than to make Germany free and happy once more.'[12] And even the efforts and setbacks during the struggle for power are theologically integrated. Hitler speaks of 'the feeling that the hand of the Lord had to strike us to make us ready for this, the greatest inner good fortune there is, the good fortune of mutual understanding within one's own people.'[13]

Again and again throughout the next years Hitler strikes up, virtually like a chorus, the idea of Providence that has allegedly 'blessed the struggle'. 'Heaven and Providence have blessed our efforts,' says Hitler on 1 May 1935 on the occasion of the return of the Saar, 'and when I take stock of the result today, I must thank Heaven, for it blessed the struggle and blessed it again and again. The struggle has not been in vain.'[14] It is precisely this 'party narrative'[15] of the laborious ascent, ultimate victory, and successful workings of the NSDAP that Hitler repeats stereotypically over many years. And this is always done through recourse to said 'Providence' which legitimized this path through his success.

A speech held at the *Gauparteitag* Mainfranken in Würzburg on 27 June 1937 can be seen as exemplary for these years in the way it makes use of theological schemata in its argument, especially in front of party comrades, that is, in front of the people Hitler felt especially close to. The idea of Providence figures in it, as it had done before 1933, but now it is fully applied to the National Socialist movement without reserve; it is its key enabling category:

> As weak as the individual may ultimately be in his character and actions as a whole, when compared to Almighty Providence and its will, he becomes just as infinitely strong the instant he acts in accordance with this Providence. Then there will rain upon him the power that has distinguished all great phenomena of this world. And when I look back on the five years behind us, I cannot help but say: this has not been the work of man alone. Had Providence not guided us, I surely would often have been unable to follow these dizzying paths. That is something our critics above all should know. At the bottom of our hearts, we National Socialist are devout! We have no choice: no one can make national or world history if his deeds and abilities are not blessed by Providence.[16]

And only a few weeks earlier Hitler had adjudged:

> We, therefore, go our way into the future with the deepest belief in God. Would all we have achieved been possible had Providence not helped us? I know that the fruits of human labor are hard-won and transitory if they are not blessed by the Omnipotent. Work such as ours which has received the blessings of the Omnipotent can never again be undone by mere mortals.[17]

The structure of Hitler's idea of Providence becomes visible here. With its help, Hitler relieves his own political project of the banality of political struggle and situates it within a 'religious field'. Its distinguishing mark: nothing within it is destructible by man. The apparent gesture of humility – 'deepest belief in God', 'Would all we have achieved been possible had Providence not helped us?'– shows itself to be a radical strategy of immunisation towards any criticism. Anything that is so successful has to be God's will and plan, whoever rises against it, is not rising against Hitler, but against God.

The brilliant early successes of the War, of course, reinforced Hitler's use of the idea of Providence in relation to his own movement as well as to himself. To Hitler's mind the fact that Poland 'was militarily beaten in an unbelievable ten days, was destroyed in eighteen days, and was forced to finally capitulate in thirty days' was not only an extraordinary military achievement. Hitler realises 'home much Providence has helped us here. It has allowed our plans to ripen fully and has visibly blessed their fruits. Otherwise, this work could not have succeeded in such a short time. Hence, we believe that Providence willed what has come to pass.'[18]

So Hitler also attributes the failed assassination attempts of the Bürgerbräukeller – 'I am completely calm now. That I left the Bürgerbräu earlier than usual is a confirmation that Providence wishes me to attain my goals.'[19] – and 20 July 1944 directly to 'Providence':

> Germany's fate, had this attempt today succeeded, can only be imagined by a very few people. I am grateful to Providence and my Creator not because He preserved my life—my life is nothing other than care and work for my Volk—but because He gave me the opportunity to continue bearing these cares and too [sic] persevere in my work, as best as I can before my conscience. [. . .] I also regard this as the warning finger of Providence that I must continue my work and, therefore, I shall continue my work![20]

In 1932 Hitler had already ascribed his survival of World War I to 'Providence' and connected it directly with his decision to go into politics: 'I might have perished like millions of my comrades. I took my life back from Providence as a gift and swore to myself to dedicate this life to the Volk. And I will adhere to this until my dying breath.'[21] Hitler is certain: 'If I have a destiny, then I am here by virtue of a higher power.'[22]

'Providence' in Times of Defeat: 'If I have a destiny, then I am here by virtue of a higher power.'

But how does Hitler process the defeats of the later war years? If success constitutes the providential character of the National Socialist project, then failure must consequently turn into a critique of the subsumption of this project into divine Providence. Thus, the fact that Hitler does not take the increasingly catastrophic defeats of the National Socialist State as occasion to revise his concept of Providence demonstrates how central it is to his discourse. It determines his actions too strongly; it is too important a legitimizing category, above all, probably, also for Hitler himself.

Rather, Hitler incorporates the defeats of the war, figured as necessary trials sent by 'Providence', into what has since Hitler's own ideological beginnings been an essentially stable system. It must simply be accepted, says Hitler in a proclamation made on 12 November 1944 'that Providence in the end helps only him who does not despair and takes up the struggle [wholeheartedly (R.P.)] against the adversities of the time'. Thus Hitler turns the idea of Providence from a legitimizing concept based on success into a concept for mobilization based on struggle and its challenges.

The context of this passage shows that behind Hitler's idea of Providence lies a notion of God, a albeit vague one.. Here he says,

> Insofar as the Almighty opened our eyes in order to grant us insight into the laws of His rule, in accordance with the limited capabilities of us human beings, we recognize the incorruptible justice which gives life as a final reward only to those who are willing and ready to give a life for a life.[23]

According to Hitler, 'Providence' was sending the present trials to 'try' men 'for what they are worth. It thereby decides whether they deserve life or death.'[24] And in recourse to the aforementioned 'party narrative' that was stylized akin to the gospel and continuously repeated, Hitler 'again pledge[s]' that he will continue his work as his duty to the National Socialist State. He reasons, 'I did not choose this duty. Providence imposes it on every German: to do everything and not to neglect anything that can secure the future of our Volk and make its existence possible.'[25] At least publicly, then, Hitler does not doubt 'for a minute that, in the end, we will successfully survive this time of trial and that the hour will come when the Almighty again grants us His blessings as before'.[26]

As late as in his New Year's Proclamation for the year 1945 Hitler implores 'Providence' for 'a merciful appreciation' of the German 'struggle':[27]

> Whomever Providence subjects to so many trials, it has destined fort he greatest things! [. . .] In this hour, as the spokesman of Greater Germany, I therefore wish to make the solemn avowal before the Almighty that we will loyally and unshakably fulfill our duty also in the new year, in the firm belief that honor will come when the victory will favor for good the one who is most worthy of it, the Greater German Reich![28]

Summary and classification

The idea of Providence, which can be traced through Hitler's discourse from the start, evidently gains significance over time and in conjunction with Hitler's successes. Hitler ties it to his own biography and his National Socialist project with increasing immediacy.

The function of the idea of Providence is made clear in Hitler's theological discourse: It serves as the *central legitimising category from the perspective of the theology of history for his own project*. With the help of this idea, Hitler's concrete political actions are inserted into a divine project, a divine road to salvation. Functionally, the idea of Providence is the most important category of Hitlerian theological discourse. At a table talk on 11 November 1941 Hitler says,

> Somehow all of this leads to the realization that man is helpless in the face of the eternal law of nature. This is not detrimental as long as we realize that the entire salvation of humanity relies on his attempt to understand divine Providence and not on thinking he could ever rear up against the law. When man humbly acquiesces to the laws, then, then that is marvellous.[29]

The key feature of Hitler's idea of Providence is identifiable through its opposite: the purely 'human labor'. What Hitler does is, in his eyes, different and much more. Through National Socialism and Hitler himself, God is enacting his plans.

In Christian theology the idea of Providence mediates factors that are full of tension per se: man's liberty and God's omnipotence, the historicity of man and the world and God's eternity, man's immanence and God's radical transcendence.[30] In the meantime Christian theology no longer uses this term to qualify concrete historical events in either a naively identificatory or denunciative and critical fashion. This proved to require revision too quickly faced with the process of social acceleration characteristic of modernity; it fell prey too quickly to ideological suspicions of the interest-led securing of politically institutionalized options.

Strictly speaking, just like all terms of Christian theology, the idea of Providence is conditioned in a particular way by 'eschatology': Only with and through God will its acts be recognisable in history. Until that time, though, the Christian faith is left with the hope that God stands by the history that he began with Creation and continued with Israel, Jesus and the Church.

With Hitler this 'eschatological' caveat is missing completely. Hitler saw himself as an instrument of 'Providence', that is the 'divine rule' within the history of (truly free) humanity and ultimately he decidedly held the view that this 'Providence' had preordained his path.

Now the idea of Providence can be understood in two more ways: as an insight into a divinely ordained universal law that is structured towards a specific end goal and is rationally comprehensible, or as the divinely ordained 'vocation' of individuals within the historical process that opposes precisely that which is deemed rational and immanent. It will become clear that Hitler's theology constructs a combination of both, admittedly with a clear emphasis on the former. For Hitler has been, so he thinks, personally chosen by 'Providence' to restore a divine law of creation. This, however, holds true from the beginning and forever: 'Neither threats nor warnings will prevent me from going my way. I follow the path assigned to me by Providence with the instinctive sureness of a sleepwalker.'[31]

Providence is a long-established theological category. Essentially, within Christianity, it maintains that God holds a promise in store for this world that will not come to light only at the end of history in the ultimate confrontation with God at the 'end of all times',[32] but that will come to light during history itself in the form of free response to the free agency of men. From a Christian perspective, Providence signifies God's faithfulness to his promise of salvation throughout history. It records that God acts mysteriously for the whole world and in its history and towards its salvation.

In Hitler's interpretation the idea of Providence turns into an immediately effective legitimizing category for his own project. It is 'Providence' that proves Hitler's path as rightful, for it is 'Providence' that bestows success and it is also 'Providence' that imposes trials. The concern here is not God's history of salvation with humanity, but Hitler's history of success and later, the explanation of his defeat.

Notes

[1]   Hitler, *Sämtliche Aufzeichnungen*, 1049 (Speech held at the NSDAP rally, Munich 30 October 1923).
[2]   Just as Hitler generally saw himself merely as the 'drummer boy' for something bigger in the early days of the movement. Cf.: Tyrell, *Vom 'Trommler' zum 'Führer'*.
[3]   Hitler, *Sämtliche Aufzeichnungen*, 1050 (Speech held at the NSDAP rally, Munich 30 October 1923).
[4]   Hitler, *Mein Kampf*, 27.
[5]   Ibid., 112.
[6]   Ibid., 93.
[7]   Domarus, *Hitler*, 89 (27 January 1932).
[8]   Cf.: Scheel, *Der Tag von Potsdam*.
[9]   Domarus, *Hitler*, 274. [Domarus does not translate Volk, his italics.]
[10]   Ibid., 521 (live broadcast of 17 August 1934).
[11]   Ibid., 316 (Chancellor's statement on the occasion of 1 May 1933).
[12]   Ibid., 645 (Public speech of 1 March 1935 in Saarbrücken on the occasion of the official return of the Saar to the German Reich).
[13]   Ibid.
[14]   Ibid., 645f.
[15]   A term coined by Domarus: Ibid., 1235.
[16]   Ibid., 908.
[17]   Ibid. 700 (Speech on 6 June 1937).

[18] Ibid., 1874 (Speech held on 8 November 1939 at the Löwenbräukeller in commemoration of the November 1923 Putsch).

[19] Ibid., 1876 (Hitler's statement after the assassination attempt at the Bürgerbräu, 8 November 1939).

[20] Ibid., 2128f (radio broadcast on the evening of 20 July 1944).

[21] Ibid., 171 (Speech of 25 October 1932 in Pasewalk).

[22] Hitler, *Monologe*, 303 (table talk 27 February 1942). In any case, if Hans Blumenberg's thesis of 'forcing the convergence of life time and universal time' applies as a structural factor in Hitler's life as 'his final atrocity' (Blumenberg, *Lebenszeit und Weltzeit*, 80), then it has its origin in Hitler's messianic self-attribution.

[23] Domarus, *Hitler*, 2964.

[24] Ibid., 2967.

[25] Ibid., 2970–1.

[26] Ibid., 2971.

[27] Ibid., 2990 (New Year's Proclamation to the German people, 1 January 1945).

[28] Ibid., 2993.

[29] Hitler, *Monologe*, 135 (table talk 11 November 1941).

[30] The idea of Providence is currently receiving renewed attention from theology after long years of neglect. See the following recent publications: Danz, *Wirken Gottes*; Schrage, *Vorsehung Gottes*; Schmidbaur, *Gottes Handeln*; von Scheliha, *Glaube an die göttliche Vorsehung*; Bernhardt, *Was heißt 'Handeln Gottes'*; Kocher, *Herausgeforderter Vorsehungsglaube*; Schneider/Ullrich, *Vorsehung und Handeln Gottes*.

[31] Domarus, *Hitler*, 790 (Speech on 14 March 1936 in Munich).

[32] On this cf.: Fuchs, *Das Jüngste Gericht*; Höhn, *versprechen*.

Chapter 5

Hitler's Notion of God

Hitler's theological discourse is not determined exclusively by an idea of Providence that is charged with historical theology. He also explicitly introduces the notion of God itself, as has been noticeable in some of the previously cited texts. This occurs during all phases of Hitler's public speaking. Related to the idea of Providence in its function as a legitimizing category, the notion of God evidently fulfils another function, one that is distinct from and exceeds the idea of Providence.

'God': Guarantor of certainty

This function is suggested early on by the use of the notion of God within Hitler's political rhetoric. '*What our people needs*,' says Hitler at an NSDAP rally in Munich on 27 April 1923,

> *is not leaders in Parliament, but those who are determined to carry through what they see to be right before God, before the world, and before their own consciences – and to carry that through, if need be, in the teeth of majorities.*[1]

Here, God is figured as the final and highest authority; reference to him marks the contrast to the deficient because purely formal authority of the hated democrats. At a NSDAP convention on 6 July 1923 in Augsburg Hitler declares that the National Socialist Führer[2] then should

> not concern [himself] with the demands of the majority, but with what is necessary based on his conscience before God and the people [. . .] We have not put together a program like other commissions whose only goal is to increase the number of their mandates without considering the weal and woe of the individual and the whole. This is not the work of creation by lawgivers such as Christ, Solon, etc., but of little men who worry about their parliamentary dignity.[3]

In Hitler's discourse God appears as 'Authority of the Whole', he is the pure counterpart, the final transcendent instantiation of appellation. Reference to him guarantees the certainty of Hitler's own knowledge and actions and embodies the leap from particularity that is always threatened by doubts and the plurality of perspectives. With the aid of the notion of God Hitler anchors his *völkisch* anti-universalism in a category absolved of any kind of particularity.

This concept is fully and clearly developed in *Mein Kampf.* This is, characteristically, done above all in the context of Hitler's explanation of the 'Jewish question'. Hitler is certain of '*What we have to fight for*': '*the necessary security for the existence and increase of our race and people, the subsistence of its children and the maintenance of our racial stock unmixed, the freedom and independence of the Fatherland.*' Hitler grounds the assurance that allows him to make this claim in the notion of God. This mission is, to Hitler, synonymous with '*the mission assigned to [the German people] by the Creator* and which they have to grow into.'[4]

On this planet of ours human culture and civilization are indissolubly bound up with the presence of the Aryan. If he should be exterminated or subjugated, then the dark shroud of a new barbarian era would enfold the earth. To undermine the existence of human culture by exterminating its founders and custodians would be an execrable crime in the eyes of those who believe that the folk-idea lies at the basis of human existence. Whoever would dare to raise a profane hand against that highest image of God among His creatures would sin against the bountiful Creator of this marvel and would collaborate in the expulsion from Paradise.[5]

However, prayer is the only adequate form of communication with this creator and God. Hitler's speeches thus often also end with direct appellations to God. Prayer as form already appears in *Mein Kampf* where Hitler imagines that

from the child's story-book to the last newspaper in the country, and every theatre and cinema, every pillar where placards are posted and every free space on the hoardings should be utilized in the service of this one great mission, until the faint-hearted cry, 'Lord, deliver us,' which our patriotic associations send up to Heaven to-day would be transformed into an ardent prayer: '*Almighty God, bless our arms when the hour comes. Be just, as Thou hast always been just. Judge now if we deserve our freedom. Lord, bless our struggle.*'[6]

The plea to the 'Almighty' to 'bless' the struggle, returns in the speeches of the established 'Führer'. Kershaw rightly notes that during his entire time, Hitler 'often concluded major speeches [...] with an appeal to the Almighty'[7] to bless his work. This was the case, for example, in the major radio broadcast shortly after the 'seizure of power' that, admittedly, amounted more to a handover of power by the conservative right-wing nationalist political elites to Hitler. Hitler both opens and closes his speech with a reference to God. He begins:

> More than fourteen years have passed since that ill-fated day when, blinded by promises at home and abroad, the German Volk lost sight of the most valuable assets of our past and of our Reich, its honor and its freedom, and thus lost everything. Since those days of treachery, the Almighty has withheld His blessing from our Volk. Dissension and hatred have made their way into our midst.[8]

And he closes as follows:

> True to the order of the Field Marshal, we shall begin. May Almighty God look mercifully upon our work, lead our will on the right path, bless our wisdom, and reward us with the confidence of our Volk. We are not fighting for ourselves, but for Germany![9]

This pattern stays identical until the end. It can be found again, now upgraded to a solemn promise, in Hitler's New Year's address 1945, when he had already lost everything:

> I cannot close this appeal without thanking the Lord for the help that He always allowed the leadership and the Volk to find, as well as for the power He gave us to be stronger than misery and danger. If I also thank Him for my rescue, then I do sonly because through it I am happy to be able to continue dedicating my life to the service of the Volk. In this hour, as the spokesman of Greater Germany, I therefore wish to make the solemn avowal before the Almighty that we will loyally and unshakably fulfill our duty also in the new year, in the firm belief that the hour will come when the victory will favor for good the one who is most worthy of it, the Greater German Reich![10]

Hitler's God and racism

Throughout the period of his public speeches, Hitler repeatedly anchors his *völkisch*, racist anti-universalism in the authority of creation of a, or more precisely, his God. This enables Hitler to justify the described rejection of '*völkisch* religiosity' once more, this time from a theological perspective, while simultaneously radicalizing it in the direction of his racist concept. Precisely because

National Socialism was '*not a cult-movement – a movement for worship; it is exclusively a 'volkic'* [sic] *political doctrine based upon racial principles*'[11] at whose apex stood 'no secret surmisings but *clear-cut perception* and *straightforward profession of belief* [. . .] the central point of this perception and of this profession of belief [was] the maintenance and hence the security for the future of a being formed by God,' says Hitler. National Socialism thus served 'the *maintenance of a divine work*' and the fulfilment of 'a divine will.'[12]

The aforementioned speech held in 1937 at the Gauparteitag Mainfranken in Würzburg illustrates how Hitler relates this, that is, his notion of God to that category which otherwise centrally determines Hitler's thought and functions as a kind of 'god-term' within it: 'the German people'. Hitler significantly relates the notion of God and 'the German people' to each other. 'We German National Socialists believe in nothing on this earth – besides our Lord God in heaven – except our German Volk.' And Hitler continues:

> I am well aware of what a human being can accomplish and where his limits lie, but it is my conviction that the human beings God created also wish to lead their lives modeled after the will of the Almighty. God did not create the peoples so that they might deliver themselves up to foolishness and be pulped soft and ruined by it, but that they might preserve themselves as He created them! Because we support their preservation in their original, God-given form, we believe our actions correspond to the will of the Almighty.[13]

Three years later, in 1940 and thus already during the war, Hitler no longer has to hide the consequences of his theological approach when he finally formulates the derivation of the aims of his actions from a strictly transcendental entity much more aggressively in a speech given on the occasion of the twentieth anniversary of the proclamation of the party programme:

> The Lord Almighty assuredly did not create this earth for the English exclusively! The Lord Almighty has assuredly not provided that a few small races, which cannot supply their own people with basic necessities, should subjugate three quarters of the earth and condemn all other peoples to starvation.[14]

Hitler sees himself as the appointed, the chosen upholder or even better than that, the restorer of the 'natural' order of creation as it was originally created and thus intended by God. Within this order the Aryan, the German, was nominated to be the head of all peoples and ultimately to dominate the world. Even though Hitler sometimes disguises his ambitions to world domination in a rhetoric of equality charged with resentment, the fact that it is the Aryan who calls the shots shines through.

'God' and 'Providence': Their relation

Hitler's speech at the Gauparteitag Mainfranken in Würzburg on 27 June 1937 also demonstrates in what way Hitler's notions of God and 'Providence' relate to each other:

> God has not created peoples that they carelessly give up themselves, inter-
> mingle blindly and ruin themselves. He rather created them that they main-
> tain themselves as they were created! By advocating the preservation of their
> nature according to God's will, we believe to act according to the will of
> the Almighty. However weak the individual person in his entire nature and
> agency is in the end compared to the almighty Providence and its will, the
> more immeasurable strong he will become in the moment when he acts
> according to the meaning of that Providence. Then, that power which has
> honoured all great appearances of this world will be bestowed upon him.[15]

Hitler believes he himself has borne

> profound testimony to the workings of Providence which stands by man-
> kind and assigns it missions to be fulfilled. And we serve it through these
> missions. What we desire is not the oppression of other peoples, but our
> freedom, our security, the securing of our Lebensraum. It is the securing of
> our Volk's life itself. For this we fight! Providence has blessed us in this fight,
> a thousand times over.[16]

The idea of Providence proves to be a theology of history variation of the specifically Hitlerian notion of God that is operational and hence functionally of
primary, but systematically only of secondary relevance. Hitler reconstructs
its key characteristics in a kind of 'natural theology' comprised of his basic
racist assumptions. However, here he at least ostensibly has to express them as
egalitarian. This is obviously to avoid his notion of God conflicting with the
absolute authority that is superior even to the German people:

> Here I believe in a higher and eternal justice. It is imparted to him who
> proves himself worthy of it. And it was in this belief that I stood up before
> you here for the first time twenty years ago. Back then I believed: it simply
> cannot be that my Volk is forsaken. It will be forsaken only if there are no
> men to be found to rescue this Volk. If, however, someone pledges himself
> with a trusting heart to this Volk and works for it, who places himself wholly
> at the disposal of this Volk, then it cannot be that Providence will allow this
> Volk to perish. Providence has wrought more than miracles for us in the
> time since.[17]

It is only consistent then that Hitler, on his part, vilifies the use of the notion of God by the Allies as heretical in 1941. He suggests that the German people knew

> that the war of this world is the result only of the greed of a few international warmongers and the Jewish democracies behind them. These criminals have rejected the German willingness for peace because it is contrary to their capitalist interests. Who, in such a satanic undertaking, dares use the name 'God', commits blasphemy against Providence and, according to our profound conviction, his reward can only be destruction.[18]

Since Hitler is decidedly of the opinion that he is executing the will of the divine Creator with his social project, he can declare that his own goals liberate humanity in general: 'So, beyond this, today we fight not only for our own existence, but to *free the world* of a conspiracy which knows no scruples in subordinating the happiness of nations and man to its base egotism.'[19] Hitler accuses the wartime opponents of pursuing only particularist interests which they then veil as universal, while he himself, in his pursuit of God's will of creation, is pursuing divine, that is universally justified goals which consist exactly in the German people's position of superiority appropriate to the order of creation:

> When, in all this, we look to the almighty ruler of destinies, then we must be grateful especially for His allowing us to obtain these great successes with the expenditure of so little blood. We can only ask Him not to abandon our Volk in the future either.[20]

On 4 July 1944, in front of business leaders, Hitler then establishes this connection on the basis of his personal religiosity:

> Perhaps I am not what they call a sanctimonious hypocrite or pious. I am not that. But deep in my heart, I am a religious man; that is, I believe that the man who, in accordance with the natural laws created by God, bravely fights and never capitulates [!] in this world – *that this man will not be abandoned by the Lawgiver*. Instead, he will in the end receive the blessings of Providence.[21]

And even in his last radio speech made on 30 January 1945, in which he repeatedly calls upon the 'Almighty', Hitler explains in detail that specific interlocking of the transcendent legitimization of his mission through a notion of God that guarantees the certainty of his own knowledge and the idea of Providence as his central category of the theology of history. The previous scruples have fallen once and for all and the idea of Providence is applied directly to his biography and his National Socialist project:

> It was in Providence's hands to eliminate me through the bomb that went off only one-and-a-half meters away from me on July 20 and, thereby, to end my life's work. That the Almighty protected me on that day is something I regard as a confirmation of the mission I was assigned.

Hitler is 'filled with the sacred conviction that the Almighty will in the end not abandon him who wanted nothing other all his life than to spare his Volk a fate it never deserved in terms of its numbers and significance.'[22]

With reference to the ideology of the *Volksgemeinschaft* Hitler continues:

> By forming such a committed community, we have the right to step before the Almighty and ask Him for His mercy and blessings. After all, a nation cannot do more than this: those who can fight, fight; those who can work, work; and all come together to sacrifice with only one thought in mind: to secure freedom, national honor, and a future for life.[23]

The functional position of the notion of God in Hitler's theological discourse

In Hitler's thought the notion of God as 'Authority of the Whole' is ranked higher even than the category of 'the German people'. It is the transcendent instantiation of appellation and it guarantees the certainty of his own racist concept. It functions as the cognitive leap out of that particularity which Hitler's racist ideology otherwise constructs. Thus Hitler manages to define himself to himself not as a sheer power politician concerned with a German interest in world domination, but as the executor of a divine will who is reinstating the injured divine and hence 'natural' order of peoples.

With the help of the notion of God, Hitler totalizes his, in reality, deeply aggressive nationalist political concept and gives it a quasi-universalist legitimization. In his own self-perception he thus escapes the threat that he believes to have seen through in the Church as a competing organization shaping Weltanschauung: not really processing the actual limitation of its claim to universal validity and thus to end up faced with the fatal alternative of regionally totalizing said universal claim, or liberally retracting it.

> Personally, I have had faith in the Führer for the past 20 years. And I personally live with the opinion, and believe it adamantly – it is my inmost conviction, that the Führer has been chosen by Providence, I would like to say by divine will, to hold a criminal tribunal over all those peoples of the world

that have strayed from the good, decent path. That's what I believe. And when we . . . (extended applause) You know, when one examines all these countries that we have fought until now, perhaps respecting the courage of one or the other, but in nearly all countries that we have defeated until now the leadership is wretched,[24]

spoke Karl Wahl, Gauleiter of Swabia on 8 May 1941 at the Messerschmitt factories in Augsburg. And as early as 1925 a future Gauleiter writes: 'I now believe in the godly grace of Hitler, whom I have personally never seen, and believe that God will enlighten him now to find the correct way out of this chaos.'[25]

His followers, at least, believed in Hitler's God. They moved Hitler into the proximity of a religious saviour, a divine messenger and prophet as a matter of course. Georg Schott's book *Volksbuch vom Hitler*, published in 1924, turns Hitler into both: 'the living incarnation of the nation's yearning' as well as somebody who speaks 'words which a person does not draw from within himself, which a god gave him to declare.'[26] This is also a means by which racist imperialism can find its conscience.

Notes

[1] Hitler, *The Speeches of Adolf Hitler*, Vol I, 67 (Speech given at an NSDAP assembly, Munich 27 April 1923) [emph RB].

[2] Admittedly, at this early point in time Hitler does not yet assume to be this Führer himself. Cf. for example, his speech at a NSDAP rally in Munich on 4 May 1923: 'What can save Germany is the dictatorship of the national will and of the national resolution. And if it be asked: "Is there a fitting personality to act as a leader?" – it is not our task to look for such a person. He is either given by Heaven or he is not given. Our task is to fashion the sword for his use when he appears. Our task is to give to the dictator when he comes a people that is ripe for him. German people, awake! It draws near to day!' (Hitler, *The Speeches of Adolf Hitler*, Vol I, 72).

[3] Hitler, *Sämtliche Aufzeichnungen*, 946 (Speech at a NSDAP convention, Augsburg 6 July 1923).

[4] Hitler, *Mein Kampf*, 125 [Except for final phrase: transl. RP]; [Emph RB].

[5] Ibid., 216.

[6] Ibid., 348 [Emph RB].

[7] Kershaw, *Hitler I*, 441.

[8] Domarus, *Hitler*, 232 (radio broadcast on 1 February 1933).

[9] Ibid., 235 (radio broadcast on 1 February 1933).

[10] Ibid., 2993 (New Year's Proclamation on 1 January 1945).

[11] Hitler, *The Speeches of Adolf Hitler*, Vol I, 395 (The Führer's Proclamation at the party convention, 6 September 1938).

[12] Ibid., 396.

[13] Domarus, *Hitler,* 908 (Speech at the Gauparteitag Mainfranken in Würzburg, 27 June 1937).

[14] Ibid., 1936.

[15] Ibid., 704 [German edition transl. MH].

[16] Ibid., 1941.

[17] Ibid..

[18] Ibid., 2426 (Reichstag Speech on 4 May 1941).

[19] Ibid.

[20] Ibid.

[21] Ibid., 2912. According to Domarus, 'Hitler emphasized these words by rapping the knuckles of his right hand on the speaker's desk' (3224, Note 178).

[22] Ibid., 3007–8.

[23] Ibid., 3008.

[24] Transcript of an audio recording. Since transcribing this audio source, a transcript has become available at www.br-online.de/wissen-bildung/collegeradio/medien/geschichte/ns1/manuskript/ns1_manuskript.pdf.

[25] The future Gauleiter Walther Corswant-Cuntzow, 1925; quoted in: Kershaw, *Hitler I,* 263. Generally: Kershaw, *'Hitler-Myth'.*

[26] Quoted in: Kershaw, *Hitler I,* 223.

Chapter 6

'Faith': Shaping the Individual

'Victory of Faith'

In the summer of 1933 the aspiring young director Leni Riefenstahl was commissioned by Hitler, who she had met personally in 1932 and who had been impressed by her films *The Sacred Mountain* and *The Blue Light*, to record on film the 1933 NSDAP political party rally in Nuremberg.

Initially, the young director tried to evade Hitler's proposal, above all because she had no experience as a documentary filmmaker and really wanted to pursue her career as an actress and as the director of her own projects. Ultimately, though, she let herself be persuaded by Hitler to come to Nuremberg with a production team at the end of August 1933 and to begin filming. Despite Leni Riefenstahl's own, more critical perception, the film about the first party rally since the seizure of power was frenetically celebrated by the party and the audience at the world premiere in December of 1933. The film was called *Victory of Faith*.

With the help of the idea of Providence, Hitler invested his project and his concrete actions with religious legitimacy. With the help of the notion of God he lent his aggressive, anti-universalist political project a quasi-universalist safeguard. This concept ensures that Hitler's project remains connected to the transcendent – for it is blessed by 'Providence' – as well as to the general – for it follows God's plan. One essential connection is missing: that to the individual, the singular person.

'Faith': The combination of religion and the individual

As a political project, Hitler's project was located on an institutionally public level. And it could well have stayed there – and did in actuality stay there to a large extent. Even though significantly more people left the Church during National Socialism, the Christian Church's dominance did not change substantially. De facto, it retained its monopoly on presenting and organizing religion. This also did not really change during the 'Third Reich' in spite of the efforts by the regime to push back the Church's influence.

Now, it is certainly not self-evident that public state theology, including the ensuing religious practice, and individual, existential theology or the religious practice of the individual should coincide or even touch. In late antiquity, for example, these domains could certainly be separated. Admittedly, it is characteristic of Christianity to make public, political and individual theology and religious practice coincide as much as possible. This is precisely the purpose served by its specific social organizational form, the Church.

So Christian theology is constantly combining three levels in both its themes and its concrete discursive practice: the concrete person practicing theology, the historical institution in which this person practices theology and the most particular universal, that is, God, about and to whom theology speaks. According to Christianity, prayer is then also the highest form of theology because it does not talk about but to God. If Christian religion links human existence and its historicity with the most particular universal in its specific totality via institutionalized, public mediators, then so far Hitler's theology is missing a crucial reference: reference to the individual. Hitler's concept of faith fulfils this function.

The analysis of Hitler's position towards the Church already indicated that Hitler sees '[t]he greatest power in this world' in 'the blind faith in the rightness of one's own goal and one's right to fight for this goal.'[1] It is then also one of his central points of critique of the 'Weimar System' that the ruling Weltanschauungen cannot produce a faith, let alone a faith common to all.

'*What then have you to give to the people as a faith to which it might cling?* Nothing at all, for you yourselves have no faith in your own prescriptions.'[2] This is the question Hitler puts to the Weimar parties in 1922. 'That is the mightiest thing which our Movement must create:' continues Hitler,

> for these widespread, seeking, and straying masses a new Faith which will not fail them in this hour of confusion, to which they can pledge themselves, on which they can build so that they may at least find once again a place which may bring calm to their hearts. *And this we accomplish!*[3]

Hitler's concept of faith has two distinct characteristics: Faith strengthens the individual by furnishing him with aims and values, and faith leads the individual out of his isolation, creates the willingness to fight as well as creating unity. In a speech from the year 1927 Hitler very succinctly and clearly articulates this connection. In front of an audience, segments of which Hitler still has to win over, Hitler uses the concept of faith to designate the basis of both individual and State identity and the formation of individual and State will:

> As you are assembled in this hall today, you hail from both camps. There are workers who until now have belonged to the proletarian parties and there are members of the middle class who belonged to the bourgeois parties and

yet you have all come to this hall today. [...] You come here because, despite all that is objectionable, you are no longer fully satisfied with your party. That is how it is. Believe me, here, too, believing is important, not realizing. One also has to be able to believe in a cause and that alone creates the State. What is it that men die for, what lets them enter battle for religious ideals! Not realization, but faith – this is what is crucial, the unconditional: I have blind faith in this.[4]

Hitler continues, 'I understand faith to be the complete commitment of the whole person.' The final criterion is martyrdom: 'Whoever is prepared to die for it, believes in it, whoever is not prepared to die for it, does not believe in it.'[5] Hitler is convinced that the Church, however, does not succeed in stirring true faith because of its modern crisis of relativization. It can not fill the individual with the unconditionality that is part of the concept of faith according to Hitler, and it can much less furnish said faith for the State which can only be constituted through a uniform faith.

The most essential foundations for any possibility of creating an organisation of people have been shaken. [...] Where can we currently find a generally accepted root for our moral and ethical notions and convictions? At the same time as one part of the nation makes out the source of its moral state in religious meaning, the other part denies the existence of a God. [...] Very few realize that what we have here is an absolute shaking. From what do they intend to derive a uniform moral opinion if one part says, we believe in God and the other part says, we deny God.

And Hitler ascertains, 'that we live in a period when this uniform opinion is no longer present and the worst thing is that we have resigned ourselves to it.[6] Years later Hitler, sees the 'dawn of a new era, that of the downfall'[7] of the Church as having arrived full-on.

But the two successive Weltanschauungen, Nationalism and Socialism, which Hitler after all wants to combine and be heir to, these too, according to Hitler, lack 'this convincing power'[8] that is the ability to unite the people in one and only one faith. According to him, they 'face each other, exhausted but in themselves hardened and self-contained'.[9] Hitler's idea for uniting Nationalism and Socialism here is as simple as it is effective. He interprets Socialism as anti-universalist and limits it to the *Volksgemeinschaft* to which the stipulations for equality and justice apply. These however are thus limited to the German people and the Aryan race. Nationalism, however, is interpreted as anti-bourgeois by Hitler, who conceives it as the equality of all *Volksgenossen*. Thus he finds, as he puts it, 'in the first instance not only a third platform from which to watch and fight the political battle today', but, as Hitler says, 'I am simultaneously constructing the bridge to the understanding and the coming together of the German man.'[10]

Individual willingness to fight and readiness for duty as well as the collective assemblage of the German people into a unity: National Socialism wants
to provide a belief that again enables precisely the kind of faith that earlier
religious and secular beliefs lost in the wake of plural modernity's processes of
relativization. Hence to Hitler there is

> something wonderful about the faith that animates a movement such as
> this, there is something wonderful about the sacrifices such a movement
> demands, there is something wonderful about the fighting strength, the
> strength of attack that such a movement has to call its own, and it is only too
> understandable that those, who do not participate in the fight, cannot even
> fathom the nature of such an emergence.[11]

Hitler presents himself as the highest of the faithful within National Socialism.
After all, this had been his accusation to the leaders of Weimar: that they
themselves did not believe in what they represented. For Hitler this means:
They did not represent their politics with the personal radicalness and political
unconditionality that would be necessary to mobilize the individual and unite
the people. In his speeches Hitler often increased the pathos of his personal
creed to the point of prayer: 'I cannot divest myself of my faith in my Volk,' he
proclaimed in February 1933,

> cannot dissociate myself from the conviction that this nation will one day
> rise again, cannot divorce myself from my love for this, my Volk, and I cher-
> ish the firm conviction that the hour will come at last in which the millions
> who despise us today will stand by us and with us will hail the new, hard-won
> and painfully acquired German Reich we have created together, the new
> German kingdom of greatness and power and glory and justice. Amen.[12]

And from this to the aforementioned 'solemn avowal' that Hitler made as
'spokesman of Greater Germany [. . .] before the Almighty' on New Year's
Day 1945.[13]

As late as in his *Testament*, facing the end, Hitler perceives the Allies as 'pun-
ishing' the 'National Socialist faith': He argues that the object of 'our enemies'
is 'to destroy our Reich, to sweep our *Weltanschauung* from the face of the earth,
to enslave the German people – as a punishment for their loyalty to National
Socialism.'[14] Hitler's faith is unbroken, obstinate to the end. Had 'Providence'
left him more time, runs the message of his final programmatic statement,
then 'a Germany, cemented by a single faith and National Socialist body and
soul, would have been invincible.'[15]

The individual is thus left with one major task in Hitler's political project:
faith. In Hitler's theology the individual is neither a discrete place nor a religious
principle. It is much more the carrier of a faith that motivates the individual to

act precisely because this faith unites it with the object of its faith, the German people. It is from the latter that it receives the aims of its actions and the norms for action, affirmation of its heritage and its hopes for the future.

'Hitler's theology': A temporary summary

Hitler very carefully analyzes the constitutional problems of the Church in modernity. He finds them in the contradiction between Christianity's claim of universality and the regionality and limitation of this claim as it becomes inevitably recognizable within developed modernity. This limitation is highly conspicuous, both geographically and cognitively. At the same time, Hitler recognizes that 'völkisch religiosity' is definitely irreconcilable with modern structures of knowledge and society. Both conclusions constitute the premise and the starting point for Hitler's theology, his theological grounding of his own National Socialist political project.

Hitler develops his own theological framework for his politics of a non-plural social modernization. He legitimizes it in the theology of history through the idea of Providence, he totalizes the topmost normative category of his political concept, 'the German people', through the notion of God, and he motivates the individual and unites it with its faith object, the German people, in his concept of faith. This way, Hitler's theological discourse clearly covers the three temporal dimensions of human existence – the past, the present and the future.

With the help of the idea of Providence as the central component from the theology of history within his theological discourse, Hitler is able to theologically interpret historical processes and to use them to legitimize his own project. The explicit configuration of the notion of God as 'Authority of the Whole' on the other hand, totalises Hitler's 'god-term' the 'German people', which is in itself only particular, and confers it with a quasi-universalist basis. Because God has called this people to world dominion as 'master race', it may, even must assert this claim. The notion of God, as a strictly transcendent category that is ranked above even the 'German people', has thus become operational both within the theology of history (and hence socio-politically) via the idea of Providence and via the concept of faith also on the level of the individual. This ensures it has a pragmatic component.

The three theological categories of Hitlerian discourse mentioned above mutually support each other and mutually award plausibility. Hitler's achievement is thus twofold. First, he imparts his theological terms both with immediate individual as well as social value domains and thus individual as well as social meaning and importance. They do not degenerate into the mere assertion of meaning, rather they achieve this meaning immediately through the action of the individual as well as of society. It is unnecessary to emphasize that the meaning concerned is a fatal meaning.

Secondly, though, with the help of his theological concept Hitler eludes the specific problematic of the universal versus the particular that religious claims to validity face in modernity. A look at the structure of Hitlerian theology shows that Hitler attempts to elude the danger of being pulverized between regional totalitarianism and the liberal reduction of validity because of an unenlightened universalist claim with the help of a specific theological reversal. This reversal is that of the relationship between the particular and the universal as it is effective in Judaism.

If Judaism can be described as religiously universalist but politically and socially consciously particular, where the mediation between universalism and particularity then occurs in an ethic of the preservation of life that is guaranteed by the one and only God, then this is exactly reversed in Hitler's thought. His project is religiously particular for it posits the 'German people' as 'god-term'. God, then, is not the guarantor of an ethic of protecting individual life, but instead the guarantor of the finality of the god-term the 'German people'. Politically speaking, though, this project is only universal in the worst possible sense for the German people may, in fact because they have been chosen for it by God, have to strive for world dominion.

Hitler's non-pluralist social project for modernization is constitutively woven into a very specific theological discourse. Without this discourse it would not be fully comprehensible. Contrary to other contemporary theological discourses, this theology enables social modernization, it does not have to oppose it. Certainly, this was a purely technological modernization, remote from European Enlightenment's normative paths of modernization. This is precisely why it became attractive to so many people.

Contrary, for instance, to the predominant anti-modernist strategy of the Catholic Church at the time,[16] which constituted itself through the fiction of the anti-historical 'deadlock', contrary also to the '*völkisch* religiosity' of the 'neo-pagans' which remained impossible to socially integrate and was also intellectually ridiculous, Hitler's theology enabled movement and dynamism. In addition Hitler believed his theological concept to connect cognitively to specific structures and contents of the modernization (understood as non-normative) of European society since the eighteenth century, why, Hitler even imagined himself at the forefront of 'Enlightenment' with his theology.

This project of modernization, however, could remain anti-pluralist so long as Hitler excluded any universalist ethic of the protection of life and deployed the random category of the 'German people' as 'god-term'. He thus gets his hands on a category for selection that is just as wide open as it is terrible. It has to be noted: At no point in time and in no place does Hitler think or speak against or beyond his theological categories. From beginning to end of his public life, Hitler comprehends his political project as theologically founded. It is thus greater than he is at the same time as it elevates him.

Notes

[1] Hitler, *Sämtliche Aufzeichnungen*, 636 (NSDAP-Mitteilungsblatt, 26 April 1922).

[2] Hitler, *The Speeches of Adolf Hitler*, Vol I, 21 (Speech at a NSDAP assembly, Munich, 12 April 1922) [emph. RB].

[3] Hitler, *The Speeches of Adolf Hitler*, Vol I, 21 (Speech at a NSDAP assembly, Munich, 12 April 1922) [Except for final exclamation: Transl. RPohl; emph. RB].

[4] Hitler, *Reden, Schriften und Anordnungen II/1*, 207 (Speech in Ansbach, 26 March 1927). In its entirety the discourse of the speech shows that it was given to an audience of still partially reserved workers. The quote is taken from an original transcript available to me that deviates slightly in punctuation, 24f. (Staatsarchiv Nürnberg, NS Mischbestand, Nr. 115 (Sammlung Streicher)).

[5] Hitler, *Reden, Schriften und Anordnungen II/1*, 207 (Speech in Ansbach, 26 March 1927) (Original transcript p. 26).

[6] Hitler, Speech in Erlangen on 26 June 1931, 16f. (Stadtarchiv Erlangen, Hitler Reden: III. 220 H. 1).

[7] Hitler, *Monologe*, 136 (11 November 1941).

[8] Hitler, *Reden, Schriften und Anordnungen IV/1*, 94 (Speech on 13 November 1930 in Erlangen. The quote is taken from an original transcript available to me, p. 7 (Stadtarchiv Erlangen, Hitler Reden: III. 220 H. 1).

[9] Hitler, *Reden, Schriften und Anordnungen IV/1*, 94 (original manuscript p. 7f).

[10] Ibid., 100 (original manuscript p. 16).

[11] Ibid. (Speech of 7 September 1932).

[12] Domarus, *Hitler*, 250 (Speech held on 10 February 1933 in the Berlin Sportpalast). The speech was broadcast on every radio station throughout Germany.

[13] Ibid., 2993 (New Year's Proclamation to the German people, 1 January 1945).

[14] Trevor-Roper/François-Poncet, *The Testament of Adolf Hitler*, 38 (6 February 1945).

[15] Ibid., 59 (14 February 1945).

[16] Cf.: Wolf, *Antimodernismus und Modernismus*; Arnold, *Modernismus*; Bucher, *Kirchenbildung*, 39–78; Weiß, *Modernismus*.

Chapter 7

Hitler's Theology and the Extermination of European Jews

Hitler's objectives

Any consideration of Hitler that lacks an analysis of his theology remains incomplete; misses an important, perhaps the ultimate framework of motivation and justification for his National Socialist project. Nothing substantiates this more terribly than a look at the key element of the Hitlerian political project: the extermination of European Jews.[1] It is the most dreadful, the ultimately irrevocable consequence of Hitler's theology: the murder of millions of children, women and men, absolutely innocent people based solely on race attributions.[2] What is the relation between these atrocious events and Hitler's theology? The hypothesis is: The theology serves as the final justification of these events that is independent of their outcome and it does this so radically that the machinery of murder continued to operate even when Hitler himself could see his own downfall.

For some time now, there has been a certain consensus in the study of contemporary history that Hitler pursued two main goals: 'a war for living-space',[3] as well as the physical extermination of Judaism.[4] Kershaw speaks of the 'two key components of Hitler's personalized "world-view" – destruction of the Jews and acquisition of "living-space"'.[5]

A while back the genocide researcher Gunnar Heinsohn proposed a specific hierarchization of these two goals of Hitler's politics. The 'extermination of all Jews,' contends Heinsohn, 'was intended to absolve the present and even more so all future conquests of a bad "conscience" in the course of exterminations,'[6] by effacing, along with the Jews, the universal prohibition of killing, the ethics of the preservation of life that is constitutive of Jewish religion. In so far as 'the core of the Jewish faith is the sanctity of life and Hitler wanted to eliminate just this basic ethics from the Occident,'[7] the Holocaust, argues Heinsohn, had 'above all one aim: It was to reinstate the right to kill.'[8]

Heinsohn thus manages to depict the attempt to murder the European Jews as an integral element of the Hitlerian project and to account for this on the basis of the specificity of the victims' religion: the universalist ethics of Judaism.

However, because Heinsohn conceptualizes Judaism primarily as the carrier of a specific ethics and thus has to refer to Hitler's 'conscience', the connection remains oddly secondary. For neither is the content of religion, especially Judaism, exhausted by ethics nor does Heinsohn pay sufficient attention to the theological legitimization of the murder of Jews within Hitler's thought itself. Heinsohn thus neglects the genuinely religious quality that the Holocaust gains with Hitler. For Hitler, socialized in Catholicism and a despiser of the Church, the 'true religion' was not primarily ethics, but 'the humble feeling of the limitation of all human ability and knowledge', a 'wonderful human insight, a superior attitude'.[9]

Prior to Heinsohn, Michael Ley argued the opposite: 'that the primary goal of National Socialism was the elimination or extermination of the Jews', whereas 'the conquest of the East' was only the 'second goal' with the intention of 'destroying "Jewish" Bolshevism'.[10] For his evidence Ley mostly refers to the cultic character of the public manifestations of National Socialism. Its 'stagings' are

> in a certain sense to be understood as 'politico-religious service'. The Eucharist, however, is no longer carried out symbolically, National Socialist religion practices the ritual in reality; the human sacrifice is carried out in the extermination facilities. This sacrifice is simultaneously an expiatory offering and intended as a new creation.[11]

As applicable as Ley's basic thesis of the priority and religious quality of the Holocaust within Hitler's project may be, as correct also, of course, as his reference to the cultic structures of Hitler's political project, just as questionable is Ley's method of analytically transferring Christian, specifically Catholic, doctrine to Hitler's project through analogy as well as his description of Hitler's project as the equally banalized and radicalized consequence of Christian theology. This analytic short-circuit, which indiscriminately deduces explanatory connections from a partial structural similarity, overlooks the fact that Hitler devised his own theological concept, albeit certainly including the idiosyncratic use of splinters of Christian theology.

Hitler's theological legitimization for the murder of Jews

Hitler does this precisely in order to legitimize what really does seem to be his primary objective: the 'salvation of the world' through the extermination of all Jews. Three programmatic statements taken from three phases of Hitler's life as a public persona testify to this: passages from *Mein Kampf*, then Hitler's notorious 'declaration of war' to the 'World Jewry' made on 30 January 1939, as well as parts of his *Testament* from February 1945. In these it is noticeable that Hitler conceives none of his political objectives in the same manner as the planned eradication of all Jews; that is as the immediate realization of a divine creator's will. Rarely is it as obvious as here that Hitler can also be understood as the political embodiment of petit-bourgeois protest against the potential for the irrational of a cultural modernity that has become dynamic and confusing. For Hitler denounces Jewry above all as the carrier of what he calls a 'perverse' culture.

In *Mein Kampf* Jewry not only stands for exploitation and material suppression but – from early on and consistently – above all for the 'destruction of all culture'[12] 'in painting, sculpture and in music, so too in poetry and especially in literature'.[13] As Hitler already pronounces in a speech in 1920,

> We are fully aware that these plays on words, these misrepresentations merely cover the inner hollowness of his inner life, merely hide the fact that the man knows no psychic sensation or experience and what he lacks in true soul he replaces with a floridity of phrases, the twisting and turning of words that appear insensible while carefully explaining from the beginning that whoever doesn't understand them is not sufficiently intellectually educated. (Amusement)[14]

Any conversation on aesthetics and culture with Jews, 'the modern inventors of this cultural perfume', is hence pointless: 'Their very existence is an incarnate denial of the beauty of God's image in His creation,'[15] Hitler contends in *Mein Kampf*.

For the Jew, says Hitler in 1923 at the Munich Circus Kronenbau, 'is no doubt a race, but not human. He can not possibly be human in the sense of God, the Eternal's own likeness. The Jew is the likeness of the devil. Jewry means racial tuberculosis of the peoples.'[16] Even the term Jew is ultimately determined metaphysically rather than exclusively or even primarily biologically with Hitler. In his *Testament* Hitler even admits that 'from the genetic point of view there is no such thing as the Jewish race.' For him, so runs a paradox phrase, the 'Jewish race is first and foremost an abstract race of the mind.'[17]

The culturally, politically and economically devastating 'pestilential adulteration of the blood' that is caused by the Jew, argues Hitler in *Mein Kampf*,

> is being systematically practised by the Jew to-day. Systematically these negroid parasites in our national body corrupt our innocent fair-haired girls and thus destroy something which can no longer be replaced in this world. The two Christian denominations look on with indifference at the profanation and destruction of a noble and unique creature who was given to the world as a gift of God's grace. For the future of the world, however, it does not matter which of the two triumphs over the other, the Catholic or the Protestant. But it does matter whether Aryan humanity survives or perishes. And yet the two Christian denominations are not contending against

the destroyer of Aryan humanity but are trying to destroy one another. Everybody who has the right kind for feeling for his country is solemnly bound, each within his own denomination, to see to it *that he is not constantly talking about the Will of God merely from the lips but that in actual fact he fulfils the Will of God and does not allow God's handiwork to be debased.*[18]

To Hitler, the extermination of all Jews equals the restoration of an injured divine order: 'For it was by the Will of God that men were made of a certain bodily shape, were given their natures and their faculties. Whoever destroys His work wages war against God's Creation and God's Will.'[19] The end of the chapter on his 'Years of Study and Suffering in Vienna' in *Mein Kampf* reiterates this short and sweet and forcefully:

Should the Jew, with the aid of his Marxist creed, triumph over the people of this world, his Crown will be the funeral wreath of mankind, and this planet will once again follow its orbit through ether, without any human life on its surface, as it did millions of years ago. Eternal nature inexorable avenges the transgression of her laws. And so I believe to-day that my conduct is in accordance with the will of the Almighty Creator. *In standing guard against the Jew I am defending the handiwork of the Lord.*[20]

Hitler is pursuing a line of argument here that can be found in his earlier statements as well. At an NSDAP assembly on 12 April 1922 in Munich he had already said:

my feeling as a Christian points me to my Lord and Saviour as fighter. It points me to the man who once in loneliness, surrounded only by a few followers, recognized these Jews for what they were and summoned men to the fight against them and who, God's truth! was greatest not as *sufferer* but as *fighter.* In boundless love as a Christian and as a man I read through the passage which tells us how the Lord at last rose in His might and seized the scourge to drive out of the Temple the brood of vipers and of adders. How terrific was His fight for the world against the Jewish poison to-day, after two thousand years, with deepest emotion I recognize more profoundly than ever before in the fact that it was for this that He had to shed His blood upon the Cross. As a Christian I have no duty to allow myself to be cheated, but I have the duty to be a fighter for truth and justice. And as a man I have the duty to see to it that human society does not suffer the same catastrophic collapse as did the civilization of the ancient world some two thousand years ago – a civilization which was driven to its ruin through this same Jewish people.[21]

This line of argument also figures, albeit in a slightly statesman-like withdrawn and embellished fashion, in the notorious Reichstag speech of 30 January 1939,

Hitler's real 'declaration of war' to the world, but especially to all Jews. He contends that 'the assumption that the dear Lord created the world for two peoples only is presumptuous.' Every people has 'the right to secure its existence on this earth'.[22] In any case, the assumption 'that some peoples have been granted the right, by the dear Lord, first to violently take possession of the world and then to defend this robbery with moral theories', while it 'may be reassuring and especially comfortable for those in possession, is equally as inconsequential as it is uninteresting and non-binding for those not in possession!'[23]

The theological legitimization of the violence between peoples in this speech then also initiates those notorious threats to the Jewish people of Europe that today are regarded as the clearest *public* foreshadowing of the Holocaust made by Hitler:

> In the course of my life I have very often been a prophet, and have usually been ridiculed for it. During the time of my struggle for power it was in the first instance the Jewish race which only received my prophecies with laughter [. . .] To-day I will once more be a prophet: If the international Jewish financiers in and outside Europe should succeed in plunging the nations once more into a world war, then the result will not be the bolshevization of the earth, and thus the victory of Jewry, but *the annihilation of the Jewish race in Europe!*[24]

In his *Testament* from February 1945 Hitler chooses this one of all his speeches to look back to – one of the very few references to the past he still allows himself:

> I have always been absolutely fair in my dealings with the Jews. On the eve of war, I gave them one final warning. I told them that, if they precipitated another war, they would not be spared and that I would exterminate the vermin throughout Europe, and this time once and for all.[25]

He speaks of their 'pride [as] members of the Chosen Race'[26] and closes the commentary on the Jewish people, now, shortly before the collapse of his Reich, in the face of a shattered Europe and millions of murdered Jews, with the unbelievable words, 'Well, we have lanced the Jewish abscess; and the world of the future will be eternally grateful to us.'[27] The murdering of Jews, clearly that was what Hitler remained truly proud of even at his downfall.

But Hitler doesn't only believe that with the genocide of the Jews he is fulfilling the 'work of the Lord'. Similarly to the Church, Judaism is an object of analysis and an object lesson for him. It is with the help of Judaism, of all things, that Hitler develops his theory concerning the connection between politics and religion. For in *Mein Kampf* Hitler describes Judaism as effecting a specific shift: a shift from the political to the religious. He contends that Judaism is not really a religion at all but masks a political will to world domination.

The 'very existence' of Jews, so contends Hitler, is 'founded on one great lie, namely that they are a religious community, whereas in reality they are a race? And what a race!'[28] For Hitler, Jewry

> has always been a nation of a definite racial character and never differentiated merely by the fact of belonging to a certain religion. At a very early date, urged on by the desire to make their way in the world, the Jews began to cast about for a means whereby they might distract such attention as might prove inconvenient for them. What could be more effective and at the same time more above suspicion than to borrow and utilize the idea of the religious community? Here also everything is copied, or rather stolen: for the Jew could not possess any religious institution which had developed out of his own consciousness, seeing that he lacks every kind of idealism. [. . .] On this first and fundamental lie, the purpose of which is to make people believe that Jewry is not a nation but a religion, other lies are subsequently based.[29]

The reversal of particularism and universalism

For Hitler Judaism represents the exact foil to his project. If National Socialism is primarily a political venture to him, albeit grounded in theological legitimization, then Judaism is a (seemingly) religious reality that actually serves purely political objectives. Hitler analyzes his greatest enemies in terms of the key theme for his own project: the relation of the religious to the political. It is also and especially because, according to Hitler, 'the Jews' are 'lying' in this respect that he is obliged to fight them:

> One of the most ingenious tricks ever devised has been that of the sailing of the Jewish ship-of-state under the flag of Religion and thus securing that tolerance which Aryans are always ready to grant to different religious faiths. But the Mosaic Law is really nothing else than the doctrine of the preservation of the Jewish race. Therefore this Law takes in all spheres of sociological, political and economic science which have a bearing on the main end in view.[30]

Now this reversal of surface and 'true core' does occur, but it happens inversely: Hitler's project is (apparently) a religious undertaking that in reality serves political objectives (of world domination), while Judaism is constituted as a societal phenomenon whose legitimizing roots provide a specific religion. Contrary to Hitler's charges, however, this religion is not at all particularist and racist in its beliefs, but is universalist and anti-racist. Particularist and racist much more aptly describe Hitler's theology. Hitler accuses Jews of doing what he himself does: religiously justifying a racist particularist claim to world dominion.

This demonstrates a specific reversal of universalism and particularism in the field of tension between politics and religion. Judaism is universalist in terms of religion, but in terms of politics and society it is consciously particularist. The mediation of universalism and particularism occurs through an ethics of preserving the life of all humans which is guaranteed by the single, universal God. The notion of God does not become effective in a totalitarian but in an anti-totalitarian manner because it connects with the individual, as whose likeness every human without exception has to count.[31] It is precisely this likeness to God that Hitler then denies some humans, foremost of which the Jews. Hitler does not fight Jews by generally denying their central belief, the fact that man is created in God's own likeness, but by exempting them, of all people, from this likeness.

The religious horizon that Judaism opens up for its politics, with its universal God who preserves life and the belief that man is created in God's own likeness, is not simply destroyed by Hitler, rather it is seriously modified. Hitler's project, too, does not purely exploit religious forms and rites but possesses a genuinely theological framework which Hitler develops in direct opposition to that of his foremost enemy, the Jews, and in which he does what he charges them with doing.

Hitler's theology establishes the broadest frame for an anti-universalist racism that does one thing above all: discriminate. Its principle is selection: 'Fate has chosen our race to carry culture for eternity. [. . .] We must thank God for this grace. [. . .] *God created peoples but not classes.*'[32] Hitler correlates *völkisch* entities with the Creator within Creation, not the individual. Unlike in Christianity and Judaism where all peoples of all men are equally worthy (or unworthy and in need of mercy) before God, these peoples have been ranked by God. And this rank is headed by the 'Aryan'.

Judaism is universalist in terms of religion, but in terms of politics and society it is consciously particularist. The mediation between universalism and particularism occurs through an ethics of the preservation of life which is guaranteed by the one, universal God. Hitler reverses this: His project is particularist in terms of religion, for it posits the 'German people' as god-term where God is not the guarantor of an ethics of the preservation of individual life but functions as the guarantor of the ultimate validity of this god-term, 'German people', as well as its claims to domination. Politically speaking, though, this project is universalist in the worst possible way, for the German people may- even has to, because it has been chosen for it by God – strive for world domination.

However, this also shows: the theological legitimization of the Holocaust is not a singular line of argument within Hitler's thought that developed as a quasi-inverse version of the (also) religious nature of Judaism. It is much more the fatal consequence of Hitler's theological line of argument overall. At no point and in no place in his discourse does Hitler think or speak against or even just slightly outside of his theological categories. Consistently from beginning to end of his public life Hitler conceives his political project as theologically grounded, especially with respect to its worst consequence: the murder of European Jewry.

Intimacy and universalism: Hitler's depravity

Hitler wanted to 'save' the world, or at the very least Germany and Europe, by driving Jews out of Germany, Europe and ultimately the world, that is, by exterminating them. Then, contended Hitler, that united, sheltering, and harmonious '*Volksgemeinschaft*' that he yearned for would come into being. He could not support this with experience, so he had to justify it. He does this in three directions.

For one, in terms of racist biology: The Jew

poisons the blood of others but preserves his own blood unadulterated. The Jew scarcely ever marries a Christian girl, but the Christian takes a Jewess to wife. The mongrels that are a result of this latter union always declare themselves on the Jewish side.[33]*

'In this world everything that is not of sound racial stock is like chaff.'[34] Hitler's racism can be biologically crude like this for a long time.

But then Hitler's argument is also reactionary in terms of culture:

No; the Jews have not the creative abilities which are necessary to the founding of a civilization; for in them there is not, and never has been, that spirit of idealism which is an absolutely necessary element in the higher development of mankind. Therefore the Jewish intellect will never be constructive but always destructive.[35]

'Culturally,' Hitler contends,

[the Jew's] activity consists in bowdlerizing art, literature and the theatre, holding the expressions of national sentiment up to scorn, overturning all concepts of the sublime and beautiful, the worthy and the good, finally dragging the people to the level of his own low mentality.[36]

---

* A more accurate translation for the final sentence of the quotation would be: 'The bastards still always take after the Jewish side.'

For Hitler, the privileged Aryan who 'has been, and still is, the standard-bearer of human progress,[37] is, of course, the opposite to this.

The third line of argumentation, though, takes a theological course. If the racist argument refers to scientific discourse, and the cultural argument to the humanities, then the theological argument refers to religious discourse. All three had specific strengths and weaknesses in terms of plausibility. The biological argument was reinforced by the authority of elements of science at the time and was applicable to all Jews, but it remained relatively non-accessible despite numerous attempts at rendering it popular. The cultural reactionary line of argument spoke to the resentment of many, but could at most be applied to the Jewish elites. The theological justification, by contrast, mediated and totalized: it was concerned with culture and nature, it was not only concerned with creating a 'redeemed' future, but also with the restoration of a past that had been divinely ordained for ages, it was not only concerned with concrete success but also with a religious mission that had to be fulfilled, 'regardless of the cost'.

This is not as surprising as it may seem at first sight. For evil acts gain their ultimate and most intimate quality only through religion. Not until it includes a religious component, not until reference to some 'holiness' is made, does it achieve said simultaneity of intimacy and universalism that render it inevitable and inescapable and thus eminent.[38]

This incidentally also means that reversely the theological qualification of Hitler as a 'force of evil' doesn't have to be (although it certainly can be) a demonization that grants him immunity, but can represent a precise identification of the phenomenon. For in its ideas theology is not concerned with chimaeras but with real phenomena of human existence. The powerful passage from the fourth flyer of the White Rose, in any case, is as precise as it is shattering:

> Every word that issues from Hitler's mouth is a lie. When he says peace he means war and when he most sinfully names the name of the Almighty, he means the force of evil, the fallen angel, Satan. His mouth is the stinking throat of hell and his power is fundamentally depraved..[39]

In line with Rüdiger Safranski, however, it must be recorded:

> When historians today speak of the 'cumulative radicalization' (H. Mommsen) caused by the conflict and the cooperation of the individual decision makers and operational areas, then they are transforming the determined will to destruction into an anonymous effect of the system. In this fashion history is turned into an event and the disconcerting insight that history is at times also made by figures that Goethe called 'demonic' is avoided.[40]

Notes

1. For a comprehensive survey see: Friedländer, *Das Dritte Reich und die Juden*, Vols. I and II. Bärsch was the last to forcefully indicate the close relation between 'race and religion' in Hitler's anti-Semitism in his study *Erlösung und Vernichtung*, 370–409.
2. Cf.: Hödl, *Der 'virtuelle Jude'*. Regarding the as always precise legal implementation cf.: Essner, *Die 'Nürnberger Gesetze'*.
3. This ideology of *Lebensraum* seems to have become an integral and crucial element of the Hitlerian Weltanschauung only during the year 1922 and especially during his detention in Landsberg: cf. Kershaw, *Hitler I*, 241ff.
4. Cf.: Graml, 'Rassismus und Lebensraum'. Also see: Jäckel, *Hitlers Weltanschauung*, 118.
5. Kershaw, *Hitler I*, 250.
6. Heinsohn, *Warum Auschwitz*, 19. Incidentally, Heinsohn provides a summary of all previous 'explanatory theories' of the Holocaust (39–128) that despite schematization remains instructive. Heinsohn lists 42 such attempts at explanation.
7. Heinsohn, *Warum Auschwitz*, 20.
8. Ibid., 18.
9. Hitler, *Monologe*, 279 (17 February 1942).
10. Ley, *Genozid*, 27.
11. Ibid., 211.
12. Phelps, 'Hitlers "grundlegende" Rede', 412 (Speech on 13 August 1920). The speech is documented on pages 400–20.
13. Ibid., 413.
14. Ibid., 412f.
15. Hitler, *Mein Kampf*, 107.
16. Hitler, *Sämtliche Aufzeichnungen*, 918 (Speech given at an NSDAP assembly at Zirkus Krone, Munich, 1 May 1923).
17. Trevor-Roper/François-Poncet, *Testament*, 55 (13 February 1945).
18. Hitler, *Mein Kampf*, 310.
19. Ibid.
20. Ibid., 46 [The sentence 'Eternal . . . laws' is not rendered in the Murphy translation, translated here by RP].
21. Hitler, *The Speeches of Adolf Hitler*, Vol I, 19–20 (Speech given at an NSDAP assembly, Munich 12 April 1922) [Emph. RB].
22. Hitler, 'Der Führer vor dem ersten Reichstag Großdeutschlands', 25 (Speech given at the Reichstag on 30 January 1939).
23. Ibid., 29f.
24. Hitler, *The Speeches of Adolf Hitler*, vol I, 740–1 [Emph. RB].
25. Trevor-Roper/François-Poncet, *Testament*, 57 (13 February 1945). Hitler retrospectively mistook the dating and sets it to the 'outbreak of war': Evidently, one might speculate, the war had already begun with this speech from January 1939.
26. Ibid., 52.

[27] Ibid., 57.

[28] Hitler, *Mein Kampf*, 134.

[29] Ibid., 173–4.

[30] Ibid., 93.

[31] Admittedly, fundamentalist and violent circles in contemporary Judaism, for instance in the settlement movement, show that this is not automatically the case and that religious traditions are extremely malleable. The 'religion of love' that is Christianity also produced excesses of violence of the most incredible magnitude.

[32] Hitler, Reden, *Schriften und Anordnungen II/1*, 192 (Speech from 23 March 1927). A transcript of the speech can be found in the collection Streicher (Staatsarchiv Nürnberg, NS Mischbestand, Nr. 115, not in Nr 175 as it says in the quoted edition). I viewed the manuscript.

[33] Hitler, *Mein Kampf*, 179.

[34] Ibid., 167.

[35] Ibid., 171.

[36] Ibid., 185.

[37] Ibid., 166.

[38] Cf.: Wulf/Kamper, *Das Heilige*. On the more recent theological discussion of evil see: Dalferth, *Das Böse*; Claret, *Theodizee*; Claret, *Geheimnis des Bösen*; Willnauer, *Heute das Böse denken*; Berner, *Theorie des Bösen*; Bründl, *Masken des Bösen*. Also instructive are the long essays by Sofsky, *Traktat über die Gewalt*, and Safranski, *Das Böse*.

[39] Scholl, *Die Weiße Rose*, 88f.

[40] Safranski, *Das Böse*, 284.

Chapter 8

Church Reforms with the Help of Hitler's Theology

Hitler, secularization, and human rights

Adolf Hitler's project of a united, racially defined 'Volksgemeinschaft' without a doubt represents the exact antithesis to all the normative foundations of our democratic, modern societies. What is shocking, however, is the realization that National Socialism is not something entirely other to modernity, is not its wholesale denial, is not the absolute anti-modern project that has only to be overcome. Rather, National Socialism is the other, the darker side of modernity itself.

Hitler broke with the pre-modern, traditionally authoritarian structures of German society. From quite early on Hitler set out a program, in itself coherent, for Germany's consistent modernization.[1] Now Hitler's scheme for the modernization of German society, however, was also tied into a specific normative framework that casts a fatal light on Hitler's 'modernity'. For one his social Darwinist idea of perpetual struggle,[2] second the fact 'that for Hitler [. . .] the "individual" and "humanity" are not relevant points of reference, but only and solely the German Volksgenossenschaft,'[3] as well as thirdly what Hitler called a 'personality principle' that says 'that history has only ever been shaped by individual outstanding personalities.'[4] The anti-universalist conditions of Hitler's project of modernity now, however, have terrible consequences for Hitler's 'modernity'.

The structural mark of post-metaphysically legitimized, that is, modern, governance is the development of an independent political sphere. In the post-feudal constitutional state symbolic and actual power separate out from each other:[5] 'A separate political sphere could not exist as long as the monarch justified his power by invoking divine right or a holy tradition. Power and society were as one.' The 'sacral order of the after-world' also 'unshakeably' determined 'society in this world, its legal norms and the limits of the princely exercise of power. The sovereign's powers did not extend to the shaping or changing of the worldly order.'[6] Not until the modern 'secularization of politics' can an independent civil society develop.

This process of the secularization of politics, however, also opens up the possibility of shaping politics around a project: 'The demise of the formerly symbolic unity of society within the order of the after-world causes the basic principles of justice and society's self-knowledge to shift into the here and now of the civil society.'[7] However, the knowledge of the possibilities of shaping society, and so the scope for political action won in modernity, can now also be used to dispose of the (normative) modern idea of reasonable self-legislation.

For the formation of republican, post-feudal constitutional structures – the creation of a public sphere and the 'subjugation of the exercise of political power to the law that is an emanation of the people's will'[8] – does not safeguard it from the abolition of plurality and liberty.[9] In fact, it is only the modern liberation of civil society that even creates the possibility of a totalitarian 'subjugation of society to an ideologically determined historical process'.[10] This happens, for example, when the newly formed political sphere is symbolically represented by specific terms ('people', 'nation') and is completely occupied by these (new) representations.[11] The political is then no longer understood as a plural and conflict-laden sphere of decision-making, but as the place of representation of said reified and thus mystified entities.

The aim of such totalitarianisms that are possible only in modernity is the destruction of what Rödel/Frankenberg/Dubiel call the 'symbolic dispositif of democracy' that is the 'self-institution of an autonomous civil society, mediated by the creation of a public and political sphere vis-à-vis to the vacant place of power'.[12] It is crucial for the symbolic dispositif of democracy that the place of power really does remain vacant, that it is filled only temporarily and without any claim to legitimacy that is independent of civil society.

The totalitarian regime revokes precisely this constellation. It attempts to fill the vacant place of power by reconstituting the unity of political power and civil society under specific signs. This is done by identifying a particular element of civil society itself – for instance the working class and its 'avant garde' or the German race and its 'Führer' – with this society as a whole. A purported unity is violently established as truth via an identity myth. The political sphere, enabled by modernity, becomes precisely the base and the playing field for the abolition of the normative principles that determined the development of said sphere: liberty and self-determination of the (originally bourgeois) subject. Totalitarianism is thus characterized by the control of the whole by a part that declares itself to be the whole.

This form of government, possible only in modernity, explicitly revokes the 'subjugation of the exercise of political power to the law that is an emanation of the people's will'.[13] However, it also does not merely restoratively return to a premodern, explicitly religious legitimization of political power derived from Christian tradition.[14] This project hence requires new myths of unity. The three aforementioned Hitlerian basic assumptions – social Darwinism,[15] the (German) people as the only relevant political point of reference, as well as the Führer as the representative of the people's will – form the framework of principles for the specific National Socialist myth of unity.[16]

Totalitarian regimes thus prove to be the risk factors of secularized politics. They succeed the modern secularization of politics and the concomitant development of civil society by using the political sphere (and the liberty) it created to then abolish it under different signs:

> Ideology solidifies the real process of the constant violent establishment and reestablishment of the unity of party, State, and society into the image of a body whose enemies, parasites, and germs must be exterminated. Through this body metaphor totalitarian ideology evokes exactly that incorporation of civil society into political power whose dissolution first marked the beginning of secularization and the development of an independent political sphere.[17]

This also reveals the normative core of democratic structures within the process of modernization: the implementation of the symbolic dispositif of democracy that guarantees that the 'vacant place of power' actually does remain vacant and that the reoccupation of this place through identity myths of unity from the political sphere itself is made impossible. Any idea of a predetermined stable harmony between governance and governed, State and society, individual and whole is thus dismissed not only in theory but also through the institutional structures of political practice. In democratic societies political ability to act does not come into being when an imagined 'people's will' is enacted by privileged leaders, but when the plural civil society brings its constant process of organizing dissent to a decision. This alone ensures that the place of power truly remains vacant. The organizational principles of this process of organizing dissent are – with whatever final justification – themselves removed from this operation, or are at least relieved of the ordinary conflict-ridden discourse and thus form the normative foundation of democratically constituted societies.[18] This certainly also means that modern civil society is constantly threatened by the abolition of its freedoms on the basis of the political sphere it itself opened.

The originality of Hitler's concept resided in the fact that he balanced the constricting consequences of the anti-democratic abolition of plurality by introducing dynamic elements. Hitler split the 'project of modernity' in order to beat it on his own playing field and with his own means. Or to be more precise: Hitler utilized those elements of the modernization project that appeared exploitable beyond the symbolic dispositif of democracy, so beyond the normative foundations of this project, above all of which were human rights.

After the mutually supportive tension that sustained the unity of the social and the sacred orders had been broken, and the old unity of the symbolic and power had been finally lost, this unity could only be re-established through repressive orchestration. The fact that Hitler intended to mobilize this unity, which was established ideologically through the racially defined *Volksgemeinschaft*, but in actuality was established above all through the political totalization of the 'will of the Führer', for absolutely 'modernist' aims, seems certain.

Unlike the bourgeois modernization process, the actual carriers of dynamism in Hitler's social design do not structurally reside in a free civil society and its own dynamism. Rather, National Socialism requires its own carriers of dynamism because it liquidates this free civil society and abolishes its dynamic of social innovation. However, it is precisely this social dynamic that Hitler does not want to relinquish. If something is not inherent to the system and structurally secured, it can only be introduced from the outside through personnel and volunteers. This ultimately leaves only one authority that can reintroduce the lacking dynamism of modernization to a society formed on identity: the identificatory head of this society that unites everything within itself, therefore Hitler himself. The double myth of the identification of everybody in the people's will and this people's will in the 'Führer' only avoids suffocating all social dynamism if this Führer himself is not the place but the motor of permanent social modernization.

Without a doubt: Hitler views himself as National Socialism's crucial motor of modernization. It is he who replaces the pluralist dynamism of a democratic society with his will and in this way satisfies both modern yearnings for dynamism and premodern longings for unity. But all Hitler's 'modernisms' (the struggle for social equality, the delight in technological innovation, the embracing of industrial society, and so on) are conditioned by a single prerequisite: Hitler, this single and highest place of power, has to have wanted them.[19]

The fact that Hitler (appears) to bind his own will to the people's will by simply declaring them identical,[20] illustrates two things: For one, Hitler is fully aware of the modern and so post-metaphysical foundations of politics. His theory of 'dictatorship as the "highest form of democracy"'[21] knows the modern political field and determinedly occupies it in its full breadth. This then also explains the tremendous fascination of the Hitlerian project and why it appealed to such broad masses of the people. For Hitler promised the blessings of modernity without its unreasonable demands of plurality. In this way it really does seem to have corresponded with the secret or open yearnings of many of the German people. Society as a plurality of intense conflict was experienced as an unreasonable demand; the desire for a myth of identity was widespread.

Whether pluralist democracy is the only possible political form that allows for the realization of the process of modernization remains an open question. The collapse of Communism is an argument against it, the forced modernization of China or Saudi Arabia without any real democratization speaks for it. Evidently, industrialization, urbanization, rationalization, mechanization, and secularization are possible for an extended period of time even under the conditions of non-pluralist social formations, are hence also possible where modern civil society is shaped and united under a myth of identity. In the Western European countries these two processes were historically very closely tied together, and the theory arguing that economic and technological modernization leads to the development of an increasingly confident bourgeois middle class that will eventually demand political rights has not been wholly refuted.

What is indisputable, though, is that every non-plural social modernization project suffers from a crucial weakness: the shortfall of legitimization in its myth of identity. Insofar as it can no longer invoke the pre-modern legitimization via traditional – and in Europe this means Christian – religiosity, it requires two things. On the one hand, a 'scientific', or more precisely a theory of legitimization of its identity myth that is adapted to the plausibility demands of modern society (biological racism for National Socialism, 'scientific Socialism' for Communism). On the other hand it also requires non-discursive methods of mediation for this myth to reach the individual. As is well known, Hitler masterfully orchestrates these non-discursive methods of mediation.

This leads us to a precarious field for Catholic theology: whether and if so how this normative foundation of modern society – with all its anthropological, epistemological, and ethical implications – is reconcilable with the Christian tradition. Catholic theology and Magisterium denied this for a long time and actively supported anti-democratic alternatives such as, for example, Austria's 'Christian Corporate State' (1934–1938).

This is not really surprising. After all, it was the Church which was divested of its cognitive and normative interpretative monopoly by modernity. It was theology whose theoretical scope was radically curtailed. In European[22] modernity the sphere of the political develops in opposition to the religious sphere, regardless of how Christianity's authorship of its own disempowerment may be assessed, regardless of whether the 'disenchantment of the world' and the modern separation of religion and politics may be a result precisely of the Christian understanding of the world.[23] As is well known, the Catholic Church only made its peace with democracy, religious freedom, and social plurality at the Second Vatican Council.[24] However since then, it has become a real leading light in its defence.

Notes

[1] In terms of income per capita and consumption standards, Germany, in 1933, was behind most of its neighbouring states. Fifteen million people still worked in traditional trades or in agriculture. Cf. Tooze, *Ökonomie der Zerstörung*.

[2] Cf.: Zitelmann, *Hitler*, 26.

[3] Zitelmann, *Hitler*, 28.

[4] Ibid.

[5] This follows the clear-sighted essay by Rödel/Frankenberg/Dubiel, *Die demokratische Frage.*

[6] Rödel/Frankenberg/Dubiel, *Die demokratische Frage*, 85.

[7] Ibid., 90. For a more recent discussion of this term see: Soosten, 'Civil Society', this also includes further reading.

[8] Ibid., 100.

[9] It should be noted that formally the Weimar constitution was never suspended throughout National Socialist rule. Cf.: Rüthers, *Entartetes Recht.* Rüthers declares 'the first lesson to be taken from the reformation of the law during National Socialism': 'It is possible to revalue an entire legal order purely through interpretation', 176. See also: O. Lepsius, *Begriffsbildung.* Hermeneutics are not only harmlesss and are not simply teachings on understanding that are subject-friendly.

[10] Rödel/Frankenberg/Dubiel, *Die demokratische Frage*, 94.

[11] Cf. the instructive article by Hoffmann, 'Das "Volk"'.

[12] Rödel/Frankenberg/Dubiel, *Die demokratische Frage*, 90.

[13] Ibid., 100.

[14] This return is the great aim of the counter-revolutionary Catholic philosophers of the Restoration in the nineteenth century, for example de Maistres, de Bonalds and Donoso Cortés. But they were also aware that this return represented a departure to new pastures. Cf.: Guillou, 'Philosophische Gegenrevolution'; Valverde, 'Juan Donoso Cordés'.

[15] Cf.: Vogt, *Sozialdarwinismus*, 277–306.

[16] Before his early death the historian Detlev Peukert then recognizes 'the causes of modern racism in the problem of legitimacy of a secularized world'. 'Because the secularized no longer provided final answers because it did not offer anything that transcended itself. That is why the search for final solutions began the moment the façade of worldly everyday myths was shaken by crisis. After the death of God in the nineteenth century, science instantiated itself as the ruler over life. But the liminal experience of death denies this claim to deliverance in every single instance. So science sought its salvation in the fictional eternity of the racial people's body [*Volkskörper*] to which it sacrificed real and thus already imperfect life' (Peukert, *Max Webers Diagnose der Moderne*, 119).

[17] Rödel/Frankenberg/Dubiel, *Die demokratische Frage*, 96.

[18] Although Rödel/Frankenberg/Dubiel point out that the 'ground of validity' for human rights should then, for the sake of consistency, 'no longer be sought in the metaphysical hereafter of human nature, a Christian idea of man or an abstract idea of freedom and autonomy determined by reason'. Rather, 'the self-proclamation of human rights as the rights of political communication places their validity and recognition on a new foundation of what actually historically occurred: the antecedent mutual recognition by the members of civil society as free and equal individuals who, through the act of putting in place a constitution, simultaneously institutionalizes itself as a plural civil society. This actually performed mutual recognition is, on its part, based on the political imagination – now become political effective – of the members of the civil society who have been

liberated from all forms of tutelage and are determined to govern themselves together' (*Die demokratische Frage*, 103).

[19] Maybe it was precisely this that saved Europe from National Socialism. It is unimaginable what course the war could have taken, had Hitler been less half-hearted in his promotion of nuclear armament, radar and jet aircrafts – all of these technologies in whose development Germany was leading before the war.

[20] As in the Reichstag speech made on 30 January 1934, cf.: Zitelmann, *Hitler*, 394f, further evidence 395f (note 189).

[21] Cf.: Zitelmann, *Hitler*, 391–6. On the proximity of this concept to C. Schmitt's reassessment of the notion of democracy in terms of identity in the halved interpretation of Rousseau's formula 'identity of the governor and the governed'; see: Rödel/Frankenberg/Dubiel, *Die demokratische Frage*, 138. For Schmitt democracy is essentially the (authoritarian) establishment of this identity.

[22] Quite a different situation is known to present itself in the U.S.A where the Bill of Rights of 1776 essentially originates precisely out of the religious plurality of the new State and was itself pronouncedly religious in motivation. The United States began as a religious, but in its religiosity plural, project. Post-feudal Europe, on the other hand, pluralized in opposition to the constituted Christian tradition. This explains the fundamentally distinct function of religion in Europe and the U.S.A to this day. There, the Church play a minor but religion a major political role and here – at least in the public sphere – it tends to be the other way round.

[23] On this see Gauchet, *Le désenchantement du monde* in the tradition of Weber, Durkheim.

[24] Cf.: Siebenrock, 'Dignitatis humanae'.

Part III

Consequences

Chapter 9

Hitler, Religion, Politics:
Hitler's Political Project and Modernity

Disquiet with the contemporary: Theology and Catholicism at the end of the Weimar Republic[1]

On the part of Catholics: [. . .] a truly tragic ignorance of the enormous positive powers, ideas and designs of National Socialism as they had already been authentically laid down in Hitler's generally accessible book Mein Kampf *in 1925. We are all partially to blame for this failure.*[2]

The person who wrote these sentences struck a chord precisely because he regretted it. Joseph Lortz, who in 1933 at the age of 47 was already a reasonably well-known professor of ecclesiastical history in Braunsberg, East Prussia, was absolutely right in diagnosing Catholicism with a great ignorance of Hitler's intentions. But this 'ignorance' – or better, this ostentatious reserve – especially with respect to the theological and religious elements of Hitler's political project, had a history and had its good reasons.

In various pastoral directives issued in 1931 the German bishops had specifically warned against the 'program of cultural politics' of the National Socialist movement. Despite the partial official reconciliation between Hitler and the Church after March 1933[3], official Catholicism, theologians and bishops, politicians and Church members, remained markedly suspicious especially of the religious and theological elements of Hitler's movement. German Catholicism to a large extent identified Hitler with the '*völkisch* religiosity' which it was acquainted with from the origins of the National Socialist movement and which at the last had been manifested in the basically 'party official', pugnacious, anti-Christian *The Myth of the Twentieth Century* penned by Alfred Rosenberg. Unlike the 'German Christians' in Protestantism,[4] this '*völkisch* religiosity' was nearly unanimously condemned as 'neo-pagan' and 'anti-Christian'.[5]

Even more importantly, though, National Socialism's victory had little influence on the professional academic work of the majority of German Catholic university

theologians. Most of them did not view the shift in political context as important
for their theology in the actual, intellectual sense. Even though only a start has
been made on the extensive study of the history of German Catholic (faculty)
theology during the years of National Socialism,[6] a generalization – allowing for
certain exceptions[7] – can be made based on Klaus Wittstadt's summary for the
Catholic Faculty at the University of Würzburg: 'most faculty members, however,
did not stand out on either side.'[8]

    Thus historian Heinz Hürten's observation – noted in his brief overview
of German Catholicism's attempts at 'building bridges' in 1933 – that 'only
a minority was sucked into [National Socialism's] maelstrom' while 'no word
was heard from many that could have been taken as a theological justification
of the events,'[9] chimes with the diagnosis. The 'number of those who kept
silent, who kept their distance from all literary attempts at adaptation, was
substantially larger than that of the "builders of bridges" '.[10] 'Open protest of
university theology'[11] failed to appear just as much as did explicit statements
of the endorsement of the National Socialist position that went beyond the
'exhortation of loyalty to lawful authority and the assiduous fulfilment of civic
duties under the auspices of the general rejection of all unlawful and seditious
behaviour'[12] stipulated by the bishops.

    This diagnosis is not especially astonishing. Since the beginning of the
century, (university) theology had been, at least publicly, widely immobi-
lized and de-problematized by the anti-modernist disciplinary measures of
the Magisterium. The ecclesiastic institutions of pastoral practice, however,
had established themselves within a relatively stable socio-moral milieu[13] and
arranged themselves with the exclusivity of their internal communication.
The tensions and impulses within the Church did not, however, disappear but
rather migrated to grass roots movements – the liturgical movement, the youth
movement, the ecumenical movement[14] – from which they could unfold their
impact with less theory, increased institutional distance, but also increased
proximity to the base. That specifically anti-modern affect, the romantic
'longing for wholeness' and 'organic life' that circulated widely in Weimar student and intellectual circles – and ultimately dominated these towards the
end of the republic[15] – gained increasing impact especially in those circles of
the Church that were sensitive to the present and to problems: the youth and
Catholic intellectuals.

The attractiveness of National Socialism

It is thus absolutely understandable that Hitler's project, at least in these circles,
had to seem like a new, moreover socially evidently seminal attempt to establish
a wholly new connection between religion and the secular world. The more so

as there had previously been a marked 'nationalization of Catholicism'[16] prior to the First World War that could now be taken up again. This renders Hitler's discourse profoundly attractive to a theology that is forced to work under the conditions of modern plurality.

The promise of Hitler's project is now threefold: for one, it will restore the social and individual relevance of religion, at least it will do so if Hitler can be successfully presented as 'Catholic' to the Catholics or at least if the set pieces of theology within his discourse can be proven to be compatible with Catholic doctrine.

Secondly, a (moderate) adoption of the 'idea of the *Volksgemeinschaft*' would, for instance, allow – at least for the 'German community of fate and sentiment' – the restoration of the religious unity within the Church that had been lost through the Reformation and seemed to be increasingly lost even within Catholicism, a fact also deplored by Hitler.[17]

But above all, it now seemed possible to overcome the inertia of the Catholic Church, its existential 'distance from life'. For Hitler's project allowed the taking up of certain elements of modernity without having to accept social plurality. Thus key concerns of the anti-pluralist modernisation of Catholicism seemed realizable through Hitler.

Hitler's attempt to link the reactionary revolution of utopian anti-modernism with the adoption of, for instance, technological modernization and mass mobilization had to be seductive for a theology that was itself torn between strict (Roman) anti-modernism and the predictable loss of significance within German society. National Socialism's odd double ambiguity as the reactionary revolution of a utopian anti-modernism, whose consequences meant modernization, accounted for the attraction of the National Socialist project for German Catholic theology in 1933.

For the individual this ambiguity manifested itself as the simultaneous appeal to his heroic singularity[18] and his duty to align himself with a predetermined whole, an appeal to the dynamism of a 'new age' and nostalgic, archaic notions of the past. This element of National Socialism can be termed a kind of 'supra-individual existentialism'. This refers to the National Socialist project's ability to provide a rhetoric of authenticity for the individual while simultaneously projecting this rhetoric onto an entire people that demands total submission from the individual precisely in order to fulfil its nature.[19] This attempt at synthesizing the individual's demand for authentic existence and the collective's demand for submission was 'scientifically' secured via racial doctrine. This contributed to the belief that National Socialism presented a societal model that could reunite those areas of modern society that were drifting apart, for example expert culture and everyday culture.[20] National Socialism promised the individual authentic experience in the form of *völkisch* experience and it did this with scientific authority. It could thus offer an overall concept of human existence in its individual *as well as* its societal relations. It raised hopes for the revision of all modern fragmentations and pluralities, but without championing a merely restorative, static, and premodern model of social order.

It was precisely this coexistence of premodern ideas of order, unity, and stability with modern social dynamism and all of this on explicitly non-plural grounds, so characteristic of the National Socialist social project, that was highly attractive for Catholic thought at the time. For Catholic theology at the time had been struggling massively with exactly this problem, the relation between a predetermined order and subjective experience, of the objectively predetermined and the rights of the subject. What was new was the fact that with the coming into power of National Socialism many ideas that had previously been thought and conceptualized only in marginal circles seemed to gain the social possibility of realization. But above all National Socialism promised to combine the two diverging elements of the yearning for the (ostensible) feeling of security of pre-modernity[21] and the dynamism of continuous modernization.

Karl Adam, Joseph Lortz and Michael Schmaus: the new and the old in theology

Despite their common opposition to liberalism and 'bolshevism',[22] the great majority of theologians and Catholics took a pronouncedly critical view of Hitler's project at the end of the Weimar era.[23] This renders the 'attempts at bridge building made by the very few even more spectacular'.[24] From among the university theologians Heinz Hürten singles out Karl Adam, Joseph Lortz, Michael Schmaus and the Braunsberg dogmatist Carl Eschweiler.[25] Now these 'very few', however, bear names – with the exception of Eschweiler[26] – that resonate with significance in the history of German theology in the first half of the twentieth century.

Adam, Lortz and Schmaus were extraordinarily well-respected representatives of their subject, and in a certain sense only became so after 1945. They doubtlessly belong to the groundbreaking Catholic theologians of their generation[27] and are regarded as having paved the path for the Second Vatican Council.[28] All three of them took a critical view of the neo-scholasticism predominant in Church teaching,[29] they were even suspected of modernism.[30] They all of them, however, unambiguously opted for National Socialism in 1933, an option that they also publicized and whose theological justification they prepared energetically.

Incidentally the pertinent texts by Karl Adam,[31] Joseph Lortz,[32] and Michael Schmaus[33] did not really give their authors many advantages. Indeed, with their attempt at establishing an internal alliance between National Socialism and Catholicism that went beyond the mere dissociation of interests more or less successfully established by the concordat in July of 1933, they doubly manoeuvred themselves into the position of outsiders – both within the Church and politically. They were caught between the two stools of increasingly rival centres of loyalty, both of which thought them suspect.[34] Joseph Lortz alone personally benefited, too: He evidently owed his appointment to the esteemed theological faculty at the University Münster, which took him away from the fairly insignificant Ermland State Academy in Braunsberg, to 'his Braunsberg colleague Hans Barion's exertion of influence and ties to the German faculty in Berlin'.[35] Nevertheless, as a rule, it was not primarily sheer opportunism that drove these authors, who in opposition to the majority of their peers attempted to build bridges to National Socialism. This is precisely what prompts the question of the theological reasons for their partisanship.

Through their position statements Adam, Lortz, and Schmaus intend to exert influence that clearly transcends the academic theological discourse and moves into the realms of the Church and of society. Yet these theologians were not National Socialist activists,[36] were not National Socialist propagandists disguised as theologians, as was the case with wide parts of the Protestant 'German Christians'. The former always remained loyal foremost to the Catholic Church and its mission in their understanding of it. Adam, Lortz, and Schmaus were thus also aware of the fact that their pro-National Socialist option only became possible after National Socialism had to a large extent renounced its initial Germanizing religiosity. They then also do not forget to emphasize precisely this as a specific credit to Hitler.[37] This move away from the Germanizing 'neo-paganism' was considered irreversible.

On the other hand, Adam, Lortz, and Schmaus were not inexperienced academics who lacked an understanding of politics. The grounds for their rapprochement to National Socialism was, emphatically, the National Socialist project, were Hitler's programmatic writings. All three authors explicitly reference *Mein Kampf* and other official party texts.[38] This is radicalized even more in Karl Adam's writings. His reference to Hitler does not only refer back to the latter's theoretical program, but to the unity of that program with Hitler as a person and with the will of the people:

> The problem was not, in the first instance, the lack of far-reaching programs and clever prognoses, but the lack of a breathing human who had access to those hidden powers, to the people's secret sources of life and who could awaken them; so a person who embodied the whole nature of the people – its hopes and fears, its anger and defiance, its pride and valour. A person, in whom the people recognized themselves, recognized and experienced that which was best about them. Such a person, who was entirely of the people

and nothing but the people, a People's Chancellor [*Volkskanzler*], had to come upon the scene if the German people was to be moved at its core and its will to live was to be reawakened. And he came: Adolf Hitler. He came from the South, from the Catholic South, but we did not know him.[39]

However, with an exception as significant as it was disastrous – the function of racism – they weren't deceived by the basic structures of the National Socialist project. In fact, they hoped exactly for what it promised. It is conspicuous, here, that given the differences in subjects and personalities, the lines of argument put forward by these three authors are remarkably similar and coincide in key ideas, at times are even verbatim. In 1933 – and beyond this year, as can be proven for Adam at least[40] – when they attempted to prove the internal compatibility, correspondence even, of Catholicism and National Socialism, they were concerned with more than the legitimization of Catholic collaboration in the 'new State', more even than the simple attempt to build an ideological bridge. By opting for National Socialism they hoped to achieve a reform of the Church.

The conventional starting point:
The critique of liberalism

The polemics against modern rights of freedom was part of the repertoire of Catholic theology and academic culture at the time. 'When we summon the passing era one more time, like a shadow escaping into the beyond of the past, then it appears to us as the spirit of freedom, of independence, of autonomy: as the spirit of liberalism,' Michael Schmaus writes in 1933.[41] There could be 'no exchange of ideas' between 'Catholic faith and liberalist thought', because 'Catholic signifies a tie to the given, to the objective, reverence for all that has become, has grown; above all, the natural order of things, and this for religious reasons.'[42] In line with this tradition, Schmaus identifies a 'manifold graduation' of dissolution at work that 'began with the disengagement from religious ties' in the modern age and culminates in 'the severing altogether of the ties of thought and volition to existing realities, orders, and values'.[43]

Now, the idea of a single history of both apostasy and uprising of the arrogant subject is not particularly original – it can be found in Catholic literature only a few years after 1789,[44] and over the course of the nineteenth century advances to Church official honours.[45] The beginning of this history of apostasy is sometimes already perceived in late medieval nominalism, but it is always seen in conjunction with Luther whose apostasy from the Church is understood to have led to the French Revolution via the Enlightenment. This, then, is seen to have necessarily produced Marxism and ultimately the worst of all: liberalism. This rejection of liberalism and pluralism correlates with the parallelism between the authoritarian natures of both the National Socialist State and the Catholic Church. To Schmaus, 'the strong emphasis of authority in the new State executive' is 'equivalent on the natural plane to ecclesiastical authority on the supernatural plane',[46] 'integration into the whole, obedience' is thus part of 'the nature of Catholic man'.[47]

As Lortz writes, the combined front of National Socialism and the Catholic Church in opposition to the 'corroding fruits borne by the subjectivism that rules the modern era',[48] in opposition to all the 'outgrowths that individualist liberalism mistook for the nature of freedom',[49] had always been registered.[50] Given the Catholic Church's fundamental opposition to the modern bourgeois, liberal society,[51] this coalition of opposition is not very surprising – it is present not only in Lortz' writing,[52] but also in the writings of Church officials such as the Munich Cardinal Faulhaber.[53]

The analogy: National Socialism and Catholicism as the integration of 'experience' and 'thought'

Up until this point, the argument made by Adam, Lortz, and Schmaus is not particularly groundbreaking. Much more astonishing, on the other hand, is that another, hidden but nonetheless obvious line of argument can be found: the critique of an understanding of faith that is too intellectual, linked to a careful but distinct rejection of the dominant authoritarianism *within the Church.*

Schmaus cleverly introduces this argument – incidentally explicitly referencing Adam – through a critique of the rationalism within liberalism which opens up the usual chain of associations that reads 'liberalism, individualism, [. . .] mechanism, and rationalism'.[54] But then the argument also turns, carefully but distinctly, against those ecclesiastical ordinances of faith that define faith above all as the agreement with truths provided by the Church, where the plausibility of these truths is demonstrable. Faith, contends Schmaus, is 'not something strictly provable so that no normal thinking could withdraw from it'; faith is the 'decision of the whole, living man [. . .] Faith is not only the affirmation of a system of truths, is not only creed, but is life out of the life of the living God.'[55] Here, at the point of resistance to a notion of faith constricted by rationalism, the bridging to National Socialism takes place. For precisely this was seen as true of National Socialism, too: to offer life not a system. National Socialism was precisely 'not a system that had been thought up, it was not a cleverly devised Weltanschauung, it was a movement that had risen from the depths of life.'[56]

For Lortz, too, National Socialism is above all 'life's awakening in its full breadth,' an 'elemental wave of life',[57] the uprising against 'bloodless, purely abstracting and hence soulless intellectualism', that had also '[unfortunately

not] left the different disciplines of Catholic thought [. . .] untouched'.[58]
'National Socialism's turning away from intellectualism,' Lortz contends,
'wonderfully coincides with the principles of classic Catholic thought as it
has again been mightily struggling for clarity these past decades'. Lortz then
offers Catholicism as the 'system of the centre' that, through its balance of
life and structure, is necessary to 'fulfil' National Socialism.[59] He is thus, in
line with Hitler, conceiving not only Catholicism but also National Socialism
both as societal projects and as existential schemas. This unity will return
the lost sense of security to society and to the individual, security that arises
from the mutual correspondence of one to the other. What might be behind
this defence against 'intellectualism' could be precisely this: the fear of the
threatening consequences for identity and society represented by untethered
discourse.

However, Lortz now also carefully changes the direction of the argument
and thus the direction of the intended influence: Lortz is also certain 'that
National Socialism, in its depths, paves the way for the practice of faith and
even revives the idea of the Church.' The task remained 'that our Christianity,
our prayers, our pastoral care, liberated from leisurely insipidness, coalesces
with the living reality of the national people to from a living unity.'[60]

Karl Adam, too, wants both: to reform Catholicism through the liveliness
of National Socialism, and inversely to reform National Socialism through
(Catholic) Christianity and thus allow the people to come to know itself. Adam,
who celebrates National Socialism as the 'return to the mothers, to those pri-
mal forces that created our *Volkstum*',[61] and who praises Hitler as having access
to the 'secret life sources of the people',[62] Adam would like to directly connect this Catholic Christianity, whose 'laws of faith and morality' are, after all,
'not inscribed in yellowed folios and ambiguous symbols, but in animate, vivid
reality',[63] to the National Socialist source of life and strength, and to do this
for the benefit of both.

The precarious bridging of content: National Socialist racism

All three theologians are concerned with reinvigorating the Catholic Church
that had solidified through scholastic rationalism and ecclesiastical authoritarianism and they articulate this with astounding bluntness. To this end, they
draw up parallels between Catholicism and National Socialism. This happens
not only formally, by carving out the structural similarities between Catholic
and National Socialist thought. Equally astonishing as it is consistent is the fact
that its theologians now also materially offer the Church precisely that category
which had already masked and covered up the tension between sociologically
speaking modern and anti-modern, organizationally speaking hierarchic and

institutionally anarchist as well as formally speaking static and dynamic elements in National Socialism: the *völkisch*.[64]

With the aid of a '*völkisch* theology' (and this is where the specific idea of the theological 'builders of bridges' Lortz, Schmaus and Adam comes in) neo-scholastic rationalism is clearly meant to be exploded – not only as a principle, but in reality. In terms of principles because to their minds *völkisch* primarily represents an affective and experiential dimension.[65] In terms of reality, though, insofar as 'the Roman God', as for example Schmaus contends, dictates 'more than *ordo* and law, more than clear form', the Teuton, by contrast, 'in his chaotic struggling and scrabbling, his distrust of clarity and harmony' sees 'God as the God of inscrutable paths, of the prescient future of horrible depths.'[66]

What was thus initiated with a solid view to Hitler's discourse was the attempt to develop a '*völkisch* theology'. It was meant to be compatible with Catholic tradition, but crucially also to be able to connect to National Socialism. This '*völkisch* theology', firmly formulated by Adam and Schmaus, more carefully by Lortz, seeks to achieve its aim in two distinct steps. For one, certain key premises of racism are adopted, most distinctly and consistently by Karl Adam. Above all a biologically determinable, hereditary substratum typical of the race and the people – usually condensed in a notion of 'blood' that is pregnant with mythology – is assumed to be the existentially determining element of human life. This then becomes the foundation for a *völkisch theology of inculturation*.

All the while, the use of the category of the *völkisch* is theologically secured with an ever identical argumentative trope. Based on the scholastic axioms 'Grace presupposes nature' and 'Grace does not destroy nature, it replenishes and completes it' all three authors identify nature, that is to be completed by grace, as something essentially *völkisch*. Catholicism, however, is the place where that grace is mediated that can complete the *völkisch*-defined nature of the individual.

Upon closer inspection it becomes evident that these theologians very obviously prefer specific elements from the theoretical conglomerate that is *völkisch* racism. They emphasize those elements of race theory that they can utilize for their purposes and blend out those of its consequences that they – above all for reasons of their ecclesiastical affiliation – cannot publicly adopt. They split National Socialist racism so as to be able to use it. In doing so, the racially definable difference between peoples is taken for granted; they accept as a matter of course the image of the 'people's body' that represents a collective subject and define this 'people's body' biologically. This 'people's body' is inscribed in the individual through 'blood'.

To Adam, for instance, 'blood is the physiological foundation of our entire spirituality, of our special kind of feeling, thinking, and volition.'[67] Schmaus also contends it is

> no empty delusion when men of the same line of succession have a sense of belonging together. Those mysterious messengers, that call all our strengths,

organs, and limbs to action and thus also cause our soul to vibrate, circulate in our blood in the shape of tiny yet indescribably powerful drops.[68]

'People of the same blood,' Schmaus continues,

> thus have similar surges of emotion and of feeling, a similar fashion of rejoicing, of enthusing, of grieving and suffering, of loving and hating. Because [...] the spiritual life is built on the foundation of the sentimental life, this, too, is steeped in the colour of blood, as is religion.[69]

Incidentally, in doing so, none of the three authors has recourse to the standard arsenal of anti-Judaistic arguments within the Christian tradition, such as the theory of the Jews as murderers of God or the exclusion of the Jewish people from salvation history after the denunciation of Jesus.[70] Rather, the fact that Karl Adam and Michael Schmaus, though no longer Joseph Lortz, thoroughly share the key biological premises of racism becomes recognizable.[71] Lortz is motivated by the same intentions, but he, the Church historian, is much more careful in his adoption of the key systematic theorems of racism.

The findings are complicated further when the question is considered in how far these authors recommend concrete racist discrimination. This appears to be principally inacceptable to Catholic theologians because of the Christian notion of universal salvation. Here the findings then start to be irretrievably contradictory. Plainly, this concrete racist level of activity was by no means evaded by Adam and Schmaus in certain contexts; in fact it was explicitly targeted. Both pronounce themselves in favour of the State treating men who belong to different peoples in different ways. They even go so far as to theologically justify this level of racism. Karl Adam does this through an extensive interpretation of the fourth commandment and, cynically, by referencing Jewish law. Schmaus does it through reference from the theology of history to the status of the German people in cultural development. The prerequisite for the theological justification of concrete racist measures is the assumption that a biological, so an irrevocably determined, difference in rank between men that has legal significance is assumed. However, this is precisely what happens.

Adam, for instance, remarks that it is 'a demand of German self-assertion' that 'the purity and the freshness of this blood be preserved and protected by law.' This 'demand' has its sources in 'our regulated love of ourselves'. In so much as this self-love 'encompasses' the entire people and also 'the ranks of its ancestors and generations it can also be argued that this demand is nothing other than the fourth commandment of the Decalogue applied to the full breadth of generations.'[72] Since 'no people' had been 'more conscientiously concerned with its purity of blood than the Jewish people of the covenant themselves'[73] and 'this Jewish legal system was legitimized through the divine revelation in the Old Testament,' it could be argued, says Adam, that the 'German demand for the purity of blood' was 'in line with divine revelation in the Old Testament.'[74]

Schmaus, too, perceives 'the just worry of conserving blood purity, this foundation for the spiritual structure of a people' as 'the result of love for the people'.[75] 'God gave to each people its, and to each people a different mission. He equipped them with the necessary dispositions and strengths. Here, too, there are differences in rank.'[76] The proximity to Hitler's theology is obvious. To what extent this biological racism, including its fatal consequences for action, penetrates theology in opposition to Christian universal salvation, becomes evident in its full inconsistency when Karl Adam on the one hand assures that the Catholic Church, in its role as 'supranational community encompassing all peoples and tribes', is 'no less beholden to the *natura individua* than the peculiarity of the other peoples.' However, he uses this merely to explain that the 'Christian conscience [. . .] insists on justice and love in the *implementation* of the State decrees'[77] for the preservation of blood purity.

All the classic levels of racism, as it was represented by Hitler and as it was implemented, by degrees, into concrete politics – the designation of a people's body, its biological inscription and codification in the genetic makeup of the individual, as well as the guiding principle of evaluating the individual on the basis of his (putative) belonging to such a 'people's body' – are picked up by Adam and Schmaus (the third level, the one guiding actions, certainly most hesitantly).

Any reception of *völkisch* racism in Catholic theology is confronted with a strong counter-tradition of precisely Catholic thought: its principle of universalism that actually renders a racist, even judgmental theology, that distinguishes men based on their biological makeup, impossible. This universalism, however, was represented in an idiosyncratically Church-centred manner in the Catholic reality of the late nineteenth century. The Church argued that, based on revelation and natural justice, its competency ultimately extended to the non-ecclesiastical realm, be this in scientific discourse, in the legal field or with respect to individual and state actions. All three Catholic theologians are aware of the obligating existence of this universalism. It is precisely the manner in which they make it a subject for discussion, though, that illustrates their interest in fundamentally reinterpreting it.

What can at least be said is that for all three authors, in good Catholic fashion, the notion of the Church remains superior to the notion of anything *völkisch*. Upon closer inspection, however, it becomes clear that the equality of peoples, apparently redeemed via the ecclesiastic idea of universalism, is not upheld. Rather, the concern is the maintenance of the universality of the Church in contrast to the reduction of its sphere of influence to a people, such as the

'Germanic' people.[78] The authors are concerned with the 'supra-nationality' of the Church, not with its 'internationality' – this notion is strongly resisted.

Adam, Schmaus, and Lortz go far beyond conventional restorative conservatism. They accept, even admire National Socialism as a movement, this 'system of the centre' of 'experience' and 'thought', of modernization and anti-modernist protest, of an existential pathos of authenticity and the duty of the individual to integrate themselves. They saw National Socialism as an opportunity to regain control of societal development, which to their eyes had become chaotic and rudderless, while simultaneously prying open Catholicism's post-Vatican self-ghettoization. National Socialism was attractive for them because it suggested overcoming the modern dichotomies of public-private, reason-emotion, politics and religion that were so momentous for the Church.

Notes

1 On German Catholic theology between the wars see Ruster, *Verlorene Nützlichkeit*; Schwan, 'Zeitgenössische Philosophie'; cf. also: Wolf, *Antimodernismus und Modernismus*.

2 Lortz, *Katholischer Zugang*, 5.

3 Cf. the proclamation of the German bishops on 28 March 1933 in which, 'without revoking the condemnation of certain religious moral fallacies residing in our previous sanctions', the 'Episcopate [believes] to be able to trust that the previously outlined interdictions and warnings no longer have to be considered necessary.' (Stasiewski, *Akten deutscher Bischöfe I*, 30–2) The bishops justify this revocation with the 'public and solemn avowals' of the 'highest representative of the Reich government, who is also the authoritarian Führer' of the National Socialist movement, 'that accounted for the inviolability of Catholic doctrine and the unalterable purpose and rights of the Church as well as the Reich government's emphatic pledge to the full validity of the treaties made by the individual German states with the Church.'

4 Cf.: Sonne, *Politische Theologie*; Siegele-Wenschkewitz, *Christlicher Antijudaismus*.

5 Cf. paradigmatically: Simon, *Mythos oder Religion*. Cf.: Baumgärtner, *Weltanschauungskampf*; for the Protestant domain: Iber, *Christlicher Glaube*.

6 Such a comprehensive study is currently being compiled by the Church historians D. Burkard and W. Weiß. Of the three intended volumes the first has been published to date: *Katholische Theologie im Nationalsozialismus, Vol I: Institutionen und Strukturen*. For the Protestant domain: K. Meier, *Die Theologischen Fakultäten*; Siegele-Wenschkewitz/Nicolaisen, *Theologische Fakultäten*; tending towards popular science: Denzler, *Widerstand*.

7 The Braunsberg faculty, of which Joseph Lortz was also a member from 1929 to 1935, 'with its public professions of sympathy for the new Führer State, clearly constituted an exception to other German Catholic theology faculties whose reactions as a rule ranged from reservation to hostility', writes Lautenschläger, 'Neuere Forschungsergebnisse', 299. On this also see: Reifferscheid, *Bistum Ermland*, 34–78.

8   Even so Wittstadt identifies three members of the faculty in Würzburg (L. Moh-ler, L. Ruland, and A. Stonner) as 'true National Socialists' ('Die Katholisch-theologische Fakultät', 433).

9   Hürten, *Deutsche Katholiken*, 219. In this context Hürten explicitly refers to aca-demic theology and the fundamental (and not only pragmatic) question of 'What is the internal correspondence of Catholic Christianity and National Socialist Weltanschauung?' (ibid.).

10 Hürten, *Deutsche Katholiken*, 228.

11 Wittstadt, 'Die Katholisch-theologische Fakultät', 404.

12 Proclamation of the German bishops on 28 March 1933 (Stasiewski, *Akten deut-scher Bischöfe I*, 31f.).

13 Cf.: Gabriel, *Christentum*; Horstmann/Liedhegener, *Konfession*.

14 On this: Iserloh, 'Innerkirchliche Bewegungen'.

15 Cf.: Grüttner, *Studenten*; Heiber, *Universität, Teil I: Der Professor im Dritten Reich*, and *Teil 2: Die Kapitulation der Hohen Schulen*. Also see: Kater, *Studentenschaft*.

16 Cf.: Fuchs, *Katholische Gebildete*.

17 This aspect takes effect especially with Joseph Lortz, who was later also known as an ecumenist (cf.: Iserloh, 'Joseph Lortz'). G. Lautenschläger arrives at the conclusion that through ' "involvement in something objective" ' – the author is quoting Lortz – 'and the concomitant overcoming of all things particular and divisive' in the face of 'around 400 years of Church division', Lortz in '1933, then, has even higher expectations of the new Führer State' (Lautenschläger, 'Neuere Forschungsergebnisse', 298).

18 On this see: Tallgren, *Hitler und die Helden*; Naumann, *Strukturwandel des Heroismus*.

19 On this see: Peukert, *Volksgenossen*.

20 Michael Schmaus explicitly expects National Socialism to save the world from the plurality of modern scientific discourse which he considers to have become confusing and even self-contradictory (Schmaus, *Begegnungen*, 10). Schmaus wants the reduction of scientific plurality, a uniform world view supported by the 'Idea of a Whole'.

21 On this see: Baumgartner, *Sehnsucht nach Gemeinschaft*.

22 Cf.: Heitzer, 'Deutscher Katholizismus'.

23 Based on analyses of the pertinent election outcomes of the years leading up to 1933, Falter, *Hitlers Wähler*, speaks of Catholicism as a 'strong factor of resist-ance' (193) and of the 'strong immunizing function of political Catholicism in the face of National Socialism' (371).

24 Hürten, *Deutsche Katholiken*, 219.

25 Ibid., 221f.; the same names are to be found in Krieg, *Karl Adam*, 113–17.

26 Eschweiler, who died in 1936, is not dealt with here as his relevance to the theo-logical discourse lags far behind that of Adam, Lortz, and Schmaus. On Eschweiler see: Reifferscheid, *Bistum Ermland*, 37f., as well as Ruster, *Verlorene Nützlichkeit*, 293–304.

27 On Adam: Scherzberg, *Kirchenreform*. In her study of Adam, which emerged independently of my research and which concertedly evaluates Karl Adam's estate, Lucia Scherzberg arrives at broadly corresponding conclusions. Rather

uncritical of Adam: Kreidler, *Theologie des Lebens*. On Lortz: Lautenschläger, *Joseph Lortz*; see also my discussion in: *Theologie und Glaube* 80 (1990) 345–8. On Schmaus see Heinzmann, 'Identität des Christentums'. – Schmaus' pupil and feminist historian of theology Elisabeth Gössmann responded to the studies by Lucia Scherzberg, Norbert Reck ('Der Gott der Täter') and the present author with an apologia in favour of her teacher Schmaus (Gössmann, 'Katholische Theologie'). On this cf. the lucid reply by Reck, ' "Wer nicht dabeigewesen ist" '; Also see: Reck, ' " . . . er verfolgt die Schuld der Väter" '.

[28] Cf.: Horst, 'Michael Schmaus', 390; Krieg, *Karl Adam*, 1; Iserloh, 'Joseph Lortz', 6.

[29] As an early testament to this, compare Lortz' enthusiastic reaction to the lecture given by the Viennese philosopher Hans Eibl in 1926 in Lortz, 'Katholische Renaissance', 42.

[30] Relating to Adam here cf.: Weiß, *Modernismus*, 493–502; Kreidler, *Theologie des Lebens*, 296–318; to Schmaus: Heinzmann, 'Identität des Christentums', 119ff. Lortz, who was more clever in terms of Church politics and who, as Church historian, was also at more of a distance to the frontline of the systematic theological conflict, was strongly influenced by A. Ehrhard and S. Merkle, on this cf. Lautenschläger, *Joseph Lortz*, 108–17.

[31] Adam, 'Deutsches Volkstum'; Adam, 'Christus und das deutsche Volk'; Adam, 'Die Erlösungstat Jesu Christi'. Also included in Adam's estate is the manuscript of a speech (sensational at the time) entitled 'Die geistige Lage des deutschen Katholizismus' given on 10 December 1939 (Diözesanarchiv Rottenburg N 67, Nr. 32) as well as the unpublished continuation of his ThQ-essay 'Deutsches Volkstum und katholisches Christentum' (DAR Rottenburg N 67, Nr. 34). On Adam's political options the studies presently available are: Kreidler, *Karl Adam*; Krieg, *Karl Adam*, 107–36.

[32] Lortz, *Katholischer Zugang* (Münster 1933); Lortz, 'Katholisch und doch national-sozialistisch', in: *Germania* 28 January 1934; Lortz, 'Katholischer Zugang zum Nationalsozialismus', in: *Germania* 4 February 1934 (the two *Germania* articles also appeared – under different titles – in a number of other newspapers, on this cf.: Lautenschläger, *Joseph Lortz*, 520); Lortz, 'Unser Kampf um das Reich'; Lortz, 'Nationalsozialismus und Kirche' (addendum to the fourth edition of Lortz, *Geschichte der Kirche*, 87–93). The 'Sendschreiben katholischer Deutscher an ihre Volks- und Glaubensgenossen' (ed. K. Brombacher and E. Ritter), too, was produced with the extensive collaboration of Lortz (Cf.: Lautenschläger, *Joseph Lortz*, 310–21). As Lortz' precise share can not be reconstructed, this text will not be considered. Lit.: Lautenschläger, *Joseph Lortz*, 298–346; Lautenschläger, 'Neuere Forschungsergebnisse'; Conzemius, 'Joseph Lortz'; Damberg, 'Kirchengeschichte', 151–64.

[33] Especially: Schmaus, *Begegnungen*.

[34] Adam, for instance, got into trouble with his local SA after his speech on 21 January 1934, which was the basis of his articles published in the *Deutsche Volks-blatt*. His speech on 10 December 1939, on the other hand, met with criticism from the Church because of its 'modernist' demands. On this cf. Kreidler, *Karl Adam*, 134–8; as well as Krieg, *Karl Adam*, 133–5.

[35] Lautenschläger, *Joseph Lortz*, 299. Rome appears to have considered condemning the final passage of Lortz' *Geschichte der Kirche*, Cf.: Lautenschläger, *Joseph*

Lortz, 322f.). From the fifth edition onwards (1937) this incriminating passage is missing.

[36] Although Lortz was a member of the NSDAP and evidently – contrary to his own statements – remained a member after 1937 and paid his membership fees until July 1944. On the other hand, after 1937 Lortz seems to have undergone a specific change of heart and to have distanced himself, at least in private, from National Socialism. On this cf. Lautenschläger, *Joseph Lortz*, 331–3.

[37] Cf.: Lortz, *Katholischer Zugang*, 6; Schmaus, *Begegnungen*, 37; Adam, 'Deutsches Volkstum', 43.

[38] Cf. Lortz, *Katholischer Zugang*, 5 and Schmaus, *Begegnungen*, 37. Karl Adam is even more radical: his reference to Hitler does not refer to the latter's theoretical programme but to the unity of this programme with Hitler the person and with the people's will. Cf.: Adam, 'Deutsches Volkstum', 41.

[39] Adam, 'Deutsches Volkstum', 41.

[40] As late as 7 July 1942 a certain Dr. Kleine of the (deeply anti-Semitic and actually Protestant) 'Research Institute for the Elimination of the Impact of Jewish Life on German Ecclesiastical Life' in Eisenach writes to Adam: 'Many thanks for your letter of 4 July whose contents greatly pleased me. It reconfirms anew our complete consensus in all things essential'. (DAR Rottenburg, N 67, Nr. 31), and even in 1943/1944 Adam published an essay that clearly exhibits racist arguments: Adam, 'Jesus, der Christus, und wir Deutsche'. On Kleine: Scherzberg, 'Das kirchenreformerische Programm', 57f.; on this highly influential Protestant institute: Heschel, 'Deutsche Theologen für Hitler'; also see: Gregor, 'Zum protestantischen Antisemitismus'. – Incidentally, it is conspicuous that, as can proven by the correspondence in his estate, Adam stood in contact with this anti-Semitic research institute as well as Catholic reformist circles, especially in the Rhineland. On these circles cf.: Wolf/Arnold, *Der Rheinische Reformkreis*.

[41] Also see: Ruster, *Verlorene Nützlichkeit*, 181–346.

[42] Schmaus, *Begegnungen*, 23.

[43] Ibid., 8.

[44] For a brief overview see Menozzi, 'Bedeutung der katholischen Reaktion'. Now easily accessible: Maistre, *Vom Papst*. Also see: Schmidt-Biggemann, *Politische Theologen*.

[45] Cf. Pius' IX. encyclical 'Nostis et nobiscum' from the year 1849, where, as Menozzi writes, 'the genealogy of modern errors [was] updated – beginning with the Reformation it ultimately led to Communism'. 'With this document the Pope reinforces the argument that Protestantism, by breaching the Church's regulations, paved the way for all sorts of insubordination and that it did this to such a degree that said Socialism and said Communism can be traced back to it that had just bannered revolutionary subversiveness' (Menozzi, 'Bedeutung der katholischen Reaktion', 57).

[46] Schmaus, *Begegnungen*, 42.

[47] Ibid., 28.

[48] Lortz, *Katholischer Zugang*, 9.

[49] Ibid., 10.

[50] Cf. for instance: Breuning, *Vision des Reiches*, 55–66; Lutz, *Katholizismus und Faschismus*.

51 On this see: Isensee, 'Keine Freiheit für den Irrtum'; Lindgens, *Freiheit*; Morsey, *Katholizismus* (source collection); Stangl, *Untersuchungen*.

52 Cf.: Lortz, *Katholischer Zugang*, 9.

53 For example, Faulhaber argues the following in a conversation with Hitler on the Obersalzberg on 4 November 1936: 'In your role as head of the German Reich, you are the authority sent by God to us, you are the rightful authority, to whom, with good conscience, is due our reverence and our obedience. Herr Reichskanzler have made it abundantly clear that the defiance of state authority shakes the respect of all authority. I believe that no other religious community emphasises the notion of authority as the Catholic Church does' (Volk, *Akten Kardinal Michael von Faulhabers II*, 188).

54 Schmaus, *Begegnungen*, 12.

55 Ibid., 45.

56 Ibid., 44.

57 Lortz, *Katholischer Zugang*, 24.

58 Ibid., 14.

59 Ibid., 15.

60 Ibid., 18.

61 Adam, 'Deutsches Volkstum', 40.

62 Ibid., 41.

63 Ibid., 47.

64 On the ecclesiastical plausibility of such a procedure see the very critical but informative study by Blaschke, *Katholizismus und Antisemitismus*. Also see: Siegele-Wenschkewitz, *Christlicher Antijudaismus*; Greive, *Theologie und Ideologie*; Hannot, *Judenfrage*. Also instructive: Bäumer, '"O, Maria kennt die Werte"'; Bäumer, '" . . . weil Gesundheit, Rasse und Blut"'.

65 Cf. for instance: Schmaus, *Begegnungen*, 16: "Volk und Heimat muß man fühlen, erleben".

66 Schmaus, *Begegnungen*, 34f.

67 Adam, 'Deutsches Volkstum', 60. Elsewhere Adam attempts a biologistic derivation of the doctrine of original sin: Adam, 'Die geistige Lage des deutschen Katholizismus', 9f.

68 Schmaus, *Begegnungen*, 16f.

69 Ibid., 17.

70 The latter line of argument can be found, for example, in the writings of the Munich Cardinal Faulhaber, cf.: Faulhaber, 'Das Alte Testament', 4f.

71 In Adam's thought these ideas not only enter the doctrine of original sin but also enter into Christology, cf. the passage Christus und das Judentum in: Adam, 'Jesus, der Christus und wir Deutsche', 88–103.

72 Adam, 'Deutsches Volkstum', 60.

73 Ibid., 60.

74 Ibid., 61.

75 Schmaus, *Begegnungen*, 29.

76 Ibid., 30.

77 Adam, 'Deutsches Volkstum', 62.

[78] As suggested by the explicit reference in Adam's 'Christus und das deutsche Volk' (5), this must primarily happen contrary to the 'Deutsche Christen' programme of the Aryanization of Christianity. Faulhaber's famous Advent sermons from 1933 also have to be seen in this context. They explicitly fail to stand up for contemporary Judaism and instead turn against the disconnection of Christianity from its Jewish roots. Pre-Christian and post-Christian Judaism are explicitly distinguished.

Chapter 10

Some Lessons for the Church and for Faith

The temptations

Hitler's God could also have triumphed with the help of Hitler's armies. All weapons technologies that global powers have since created – atomic bombs and intercontinental ballistic missiles, radar and jet fighters, computers and electronic communication – were essentially also within Hitler's reach. And the power that resides in Hitler's God himself has not been vanquished for all time, either. It is the power of a God who promises salvation in the here and now. This 'politics of salvation'[1] was and still is dangerously fascinating.

At the core of these politics lies a project of purification, of 'cleansing', of liberation – however not always from my own sins or my own mortality, but from the others and the imposition that they represent. This God promises an 'eliminatory salvation', salvation at the cost of the existence of others. This is salvation from the ills of this world by eliminating everything and everybody allegedly responsible for my suffering. This 'salvation' certainly has one great advantage: it can be politically produced, or so at least it promises.

Within this project theology, that is, the discourse on God, serves to reconfigure desires into duties. That is also why it was not necessary to make this theology per se truly binding within National Socialism. For Hitler himself this reconfiguration was certainly of the highest relevance, different mechanisms may have been at play with others. Politically speaking, the fact that certain desires were shared and converted into political action was sufficient and the determining factor. These yearnings, like all deep yearnings, developed an unbelievable strength. These yearnings per se are ambivalent, all of Hitler's responses to them proved to be tempting.

Temptations are unfounded promises, promises that can be made, but can never be kept. Temptations play with yearnings and draw their political strength and their personal fascination from these. The monstrous crimes of National Socialism cover over those elements within it that can develop a lasting attraction. But they play with yearnings and hopes that did not simply disappear with National Socialism. After all, at the time, Hitler was invested with power by the elites, he did not really have to 'conquer' it himself. A review of Hitler's theology shows which answers to which yearnings are evidently awful temptations.

Hitler's project is a political project, but it is especially Hitler's theology that opens up a double, trans-political reference: to the individual by voicing his deepest yearnings, and to God who legitimizes these yearnings but vastly transcends the political field. Individual yearnings now suddenly appear as justified within God himself and thus ultimately lose the character of individual yearning. They are turned from an expression of individual sufferance into duties to God and this seems to render everything that is required to achieve them permissible, even imperative. The place where this happens, however, is the political realm again. This blurring of the boundaries between the political and the most intimate as well as the most universal is the central function of Hitler's theology within his National Socialist project.

If National Socialism, in response to the humiliating defeat in 1918, is seen as the attempt to politically implement the ideal of the racially homogeneous '*Volksgemeinschaft*' where a heroic 'master race' celebrates the ideal of battle and while doing so believes itself to be supported by an integrally religious as well as scientific 'Weltanschauung', then the desires it evoked and simultaneously catered to can be reconstructed. It was a desire for community and for the alleviation of humiliation, the desire for the 'heroic' life and for a religious monism beyond modern science–faith divide and incidentally also beyond the denominational divide. All of these then merge in one idea: the desire for self-redemption.

The 'yearning for community'[2]

Like many others at the time, Hitler shared the 'yearning for community'. Hitler's project operates primarily with a promise of security and home(land) [*Heimat*] to those who are culturally insecure and materially threatened. The culturally homogenous German *Volksgemeinschaft*, 'cleansed' of all modern confusions of plurality, was National Socialism's key and very effective utopia.

In order to live under the National Socialist regime it was necessary to share or at least to pretend to share this 'yearning for community'. Those who disrupted this idyllic community or who were identified as troublemakers paid a high price, oftentimes they paid with their lives. The 'German *Volksgemeinschaft*' was National Socialism's governing ideological metaphor, to be an 'enemy of the people' a death sentence. The precise and concrete delimitation of this *Volksgemeinschaft* remained blurred. Thus, all those outside the predetermined victim groups could hope for a long time that they belonged to the former, or at least were not excluded on principle. This is one of the reasons for the lack of solidarity between the victim groups.

The reasons leading to the affirmation of the '*Volksgemeinschaft*' could also remain open. Be it '*völkisch* religiosity', bourgeois or anti-bourgeois resentment, fear of the disadvantages of exclusion or even sheer opportunism – whatever it was that motivated the membership in the community it was important to share this yearning for community, not the reasons behind it.

Hitler's God promised salvation to the many through mercilessness towards others. Hitler's God is a God without grace. In order to experience themselves as a community, this God's 'chosen people' had to exclude others to the point of death. It longed for community because it could not bear the complexity of modernity, not least its cultural complexity. It had to rule the world in order to bear being in it. The desire for the real or imagined security of premodern times also operated in German interwar Catholicism and increased its distance to the Weimar Democracy.

Is not the 'yearning for community' something profoundly human, though? It is, and that is precisely why it is so dangerous. After all, next to National Socialism the yearning for community also produced Communism in the twentieth century. Both of these were political projects of anti-individualist collectivization with mass appeal, both of them alternatives to liberal modernity and its unreasonable demands of the individual.

The Communist 'classless society' and the National Socialist idyll of the *Volksgemeinschaft* both fascinated the masses and led them to ruin. If the political history of the twentieth century proves one thing apart from the already known abysmal nature of man, then it is the realization that, within differentiated societies, political projects that operate with community idylls necessarily become totalitarian: either by excluding and often annihilating those who reject this community and its idyll for whatever reasons, or by denouncing others as incapable of community from the start. For the Catholic Church, this message is doubly harsh. On the one hand it was suspicious of the modern ideas and pursuit of freedom for a long time, on the other hand many of its reform movements, especially, operated around the notion of community in response to these liberal challenges.

So on the one hand, the Catholic Church openly opposed the project of bourgeois modernity, the plan and the reality of a plural, liberal society,[3] from the French Revolution[4] to the Second Vatican Council. With the Augustinian motto 'No Liberty for Error' the Church argued for a concept of state that was based on the notion of estates in terms of its legal policy, appealed to a transhistorical idea of natural law, and demanded the religious unity of the state as well as its close ties with the Church. The state was defined as a structure preordained to man that demanded the unity of law and morals, legality and morality. The individual was conceived through his integration into this order, true freedom defined as obedience to the divinely ordained structure.

Up until 1945 Western Liberalism was a dreaded opponent of the Catholic Church in terms of Weltanschauung to the same degree as was 'Bolshevism'. For a long time, the Church supported authoritarian, Catholic regimes such as Franco's Spain, Tiso's Slovakia, Salazar's Portugal, or the 'Christliche

Ständestaat' in Austria (1934–1938).[5] And there were influential forces in the Vatican who favoured an authoritarian, Catholic regime for Italy as late as 1944.[6] This conception was not entirely overcome until the Second Vatican Council, in particular its recognition of religious freedom. In the face of the looming victory of the Western democracies over Hitler, the Church's real-politik had already changed course in the direction of a careful acceptance of democracy.

On the other hand, while the Catholic Church was manifestly anti-liberal, anti-modern, and anti-individualist before the Second Vatican Council (1962–1965), it was only partially oriented toward notions of community or even a movement. Rather, it conceived and constituted itself as a societas perfecta, a religious institu-tion of salvation and sacramental establishment of salvation. With the exception of select Christian corporate movements on the one side and Catholic reformist movements on the other side,[7] it operated firmly on the ground of conventionally modern institutional strategies and constitutions of institutions.

The famous distinction between community and society,[8] put forward by Ferdinand Tönnies, had certainly already permeated, in a popularized fash-ion, into ecclesiastic consciousness after World War I. The sensitive and above all the young elites in the Catholic Church demanded real shared experiences of their salvation establishment that made them feel part of something big-ger, something beyond the defensive triumphalism of vast institutions and the juridical and moral theological demands for obedience. These elites then drew these shared experiences from, for instance, the youth or the liturgical movements. It was not until the anti-Communism of the postwar era when the Church finally affirmed democracy as a social form of organization in the 1950s that what had seemed impossible became possible: the alliance of Western Liberalism and Catholic Church.[9]

Admittedly, in times during which, on the one hand, anti-liberal, even theo-cratic positions are gaining strength in some non-Christian religions, and on the other hand, differentiated societies force a high degree of individu-alization that disempowers the Church as an institution offering orientation, the temptation is set up for the Catholic Church to reactivate its former anti-Liberalism and 'not to back the cultivation of modern ambitions to freedom'.[10] It would, however, be disastrous should the Church again cater to the anti-Liberal 'yearning for community'. Jesus' universal message of freedom alone prohibits this. But it also cannot do it in view of the present. For here the fol-lowing holds true: 'Stable affiliations have become unusual. They are missed, when they are lacking; they are more or less bothersome when they exist.'[11]

Since its beginnings Christianity has known the tension between constitu-tive community and inacceptable individuality before God. Coenobites and Anchoresses, the celibate priest and the family as Ekklesiola, Paul in his unique experience in Damascus and the early Judeo-Christian congregation in Jerusalem, or even the Pope, who can, 'ex sese,' make infallible ex-cathedra decisions, but then only if he is interpreting the faith of the Church: Christianity is situated in tension between individuality and community, not at one of the poles.

Church action does not begin with community; community is the result of Church action. The Church does not exist in order to facilitate shared experience, but it facilitates shared experience when it fulfils its purpose: to be God's chosen people in the midst of humanity and to operate as the universal sacrament of salvation.[12]

Yearning for the alleviation of humiliation

Like many at the time, Hitler shared the hope for an alleviation of the humiliation he thought to have suffered by the German defeat in 1918. To identify with social collectives to such a high degree that their defeats are experienced as a personal affront is not necessarily a new phenomenon, but one that has become highly virulent in modernity.[13] States survive based on the identification of the individual's experience and his body with the political collective. It is equally not new to react to the humiliation of a collective defeat with strategies designed to alleviate the injury. Essentially, these strategies are always similar: denial, activism, and, worst of all, denunciation.

In the context of 'Hitler's theology' strategies of 'injury compensation' are repeatedly encountered. For one there is the humiliation that Hitler, along with many if not most Germans, felt so deeply and suffered after the defeat of 1918. Viewed from the present, the degree to which the relatively moderate territorial losses were perceived as cuts into the 'flesh' seems incomprehensible, as does the extent to which the defeat of the German Reich was experienced as a personal humiliation. In Hitler's biography this experience of humiliation was the key trigger that shaped his Weltanschauung as well as to the decision to go into politics.[14]

Of course, identifications such as this are extremely odd. How and why should individuals identify with a collective to the degree where they experience its defeat as their own, even though inversely, the individual is usually fairly irrelevant to the collective subject, the nation, for instance, in the case of war would very naturally demand the life of the individual to save itself. This (socio-)psychological phenomenon is astounding time and again, but cannot be discussed in detail here.[15] However, we are responsible for who we identify with and what we perceive as humiliating. It indicates the processes of identification through which we identify our selves. And we are even more responsible for how we deal with humiliations, how we try to compensate them, and how we react to them.

Hitler, like many others at the time, reacted with resentment, revenge projects, and scapegoating mechanisms. Unlike millions of others, however,

Hitler – owing to his rhetorical talent and his unscrupulousness – was able to convert these reactions into a successful political project. The 'Stab-in-the-back-legend' had already been nothing but resentment, revenge project, and scapegoating mechanism. Hitler's National Socialism brought these mechanisms to a head and focused them on the Jews in the hope of achieving an alleviation of humiliation, even compensation for humiliation by excluding and exterminating Jewish people, culture, and traditions. Ultimately, this subsumed everything that irritated Hitler.

Every human permanently suffers humiliations and has to deal with them. And the Church as an institution experiences especially modernity as one single instance of humiliation. It gradually lost its monopoly on the interpretation of the cosmos, society, and presently also of individual life, even that of its own members.[16] Through the Second Vatican Council it succeeded in establishing a critical and yet solidary relationship to this present, that had taken away so much of its power and influence – admittedly after 100 years of strategic denunciation. But it succeeded in the end.

In this way, the Second Vatican Council is a spiritual event and a request to us. The unconditional solidarity with all men, especially those who suffer and are oppressed, the political and ethical universalism, and the fundamental rejection of any limits to solidarity are true achievements by the Council. This was, and still is, also a lesson learnt from the behaviour of the great majority of the Church during National Socialism. And it asks us, who it is we identify with, and also whether we, if need be, can suffer insult without hatred.

The temptation of the heroic life

Hitler shared with many others at the time the desire for a heroic life, for a life beyond the laborious everyday, for a life of honour and courage, of publicity and spectacular action. From the George-Kreis* to Ernst Jünger, from the youth movement to the Freikorps** scene: resentment of the 'mass', everyday life, the 'flattening' was widespread, especially among the elites. Effectively, Hitler, too, did not emerge from his stultifying inertia to find himself until World War I. After the war, he staged an excessive hero worship and conceived of the Aryans as a people of heroes.

The separation of the exalted from the banal, of the exceptional from the average, of the sublime from the base, is a great temptation. It promises self-approval and sovereignty, (self-)respect and the gaining of distinction. It is often also truly bound up with effort, discipline, and courage, so has a price and thus engenders even more self-satisfaction. This also holds true, and

* A fin-de-siècle literary movement of conservative, elitist inclinations.
** Units of military volunteers.

especially so, for religious people. Heroism as an existential concept is also a religious challenge. Religious people, according to their faith, are concerned with the most exalted, the most exceptional, and the sublime per se and this demands quite a lot of them which they in turn, perhaps more so than others, are willing to give.

Heroism, though, as an existential concept – not as the answer to ineluctable challenges – disunites people other than themselves from their everyday life and their being worthy of mercy. Their hardships and worries, their joys and hopes are of no interest, in fact, they tend to be scorned. Heroism as existential concept is flight, flight from the wretchedness of one's own existence, from the efforts of affectionate attention to that which is small and unprepossessing, it is the flight from reality, from everyday life.

And yet, everyday life is where the spirit is located in Christianity.[17] Whether our beliefs are concrete and turn into reality or whether they remain ideals and postulations become apparent in everyday life. Everyday life is the serious test of our theological concepts. Do they have meaning, or is their meaning merely asserted? Everyday life is the place where our religious concepts have to prove their suitability. Can life be discovered through them, or not? Can walls be overcome with them, or not? Can they aid the understanding of foreign languages spoken by foreign peoples, even if only slowly and laboriously, or not? Do they aid the identification of the enemies of man and his life, or not? Do they aid the discovery of love and of the greatness of small gestures and things, or not? Do they furnish God with a place in this world, or not?

Heroism as existential concept tends to skip everyday life. It seeks feeling. In the spiritual tradition, renouncing this kind of heroism signifies humility.

The temptation of 'theological totalitariansim'

Hitler shared, as did many people at the time, the desire for a unified principle that could explain everything. He had found it in the racism that he secured theologically through the notion of a racist God deductable from 'Creation'. Thus Hitler closes the difference between belief and knowledge. At its core, Hitler's theology is monistic. It levels the irresolvable difference between God and mankind, between belief and knowledge simply by inferring God's Will from the (allegedly) racist order of nature which once more totalizes this racist construct. The notion of God operates as a process of totalization.

Theological totalitarianism is characterized by two features, one formal and one content-related. Formally, it makes God available by totalizing its own partiality, materially, though, it sacrifices God's benevolence to God's omnipotence. Theological totalitarianism places God at its command. One element of God, his omnipotence, is simultaneously given importance and negated. It is given importance as the basis for theological totalitarianism's own claims, and it is negated in the face of these claims. Theological totalitarianism speaks of God as if he were unmysterious, it does what all totalitarianism does: it claims to occupy a singular central perspective but only totalizes its own view. Only God can take on the central perspective without totalization. He alone can occupy it simultaneously to all other positions; can be within and simultaneously beyond history. This is theologically expressed in the belief in God's trinity.

In addition, theological totalitarianism sacrifices God's benevolence and love to his omnipotence. God's omnipotence is not one of benevolence and love, but God's 'love' is his power. That is why Hitler can interpret the annihilation of the German people as the will of the Almighty: the German people were simply unworthy of divine election.

The two operations, the formal and the content-related, are connected. Benevolence loves plurality, the manifold, the other. Through this it gains sovereignty and is free of resentment. Repressive power, on the other hand, loves exclusion, homogeneity, and above all itself. Since this love, just like the sovereignty of power in general, is mostly fictional it has to work itself up into a desperate spiral of outperforming itself.

What this means

All of this means that Hitler, like many others at the time, shared the desire for salvation, for salvation not through a Christian or Jewish God of grace and mercy, but through his own strength and effort. Within Hitler's theology, this meant proving yourself to be a true member of the master race. For that was the imperative of this God: the German people were to prove themselves worthy of its 'election' that had been constituted through 'Creation'.

However, Hitler's God saved only those who proved themselves 'worthy'. This, however, is the dogma of self-redemption: one has to be worthy of salvation. That is why this God's faithful neither require nor know any mercy. Their God is not the giver of salvation, but the guarantor of mercilessness. Self-redemption, however, is merciless. What does this mean for today?

In terms of politics this means opting for the rights of freedom of the individual, rather than the salvation vision of a harbouring community; opting for the identification with suffering humans, rather than with political formations; opting for the orientation of a body politic towards the everyday life of the people within it, rather than towards schemes of heroic existence.

In terms of theology it means overcoming all totalitarianism that turns God into an all-explaining, all-determining, merciless singularity, rather than the merciful redeemer of all people. And it also means overcoming the attitude that believes we could redeem ourselves and do not require God's mercy. It means trusting in freedom and practically serving God by a commitment to peace and justice.

In terms of individuality and spirituality, however, it means the ability to be lonely if need be without doubting, suffering insult without seeking revenge, enduring the banality of life without escaping into heroism, not wanting to redeem oneself, but trusting in God, whom we do not control and who remains mysterious, even strange to us, and whose centre is the devotion to those most in need of his grace.

Notes

1   Kershaw, *Hitler II*, xxxvi.
2   Which is the title of a book, still worth reading, written by Alois Baumgartner on the 'Ideas and Currents in Weimar Republic Catholicism' (Baumgartner, *Sehnsucht nach Gemeinschaft*). Baumgartner analyses the extent to which the yearning for the (imagined) security of pre-modernity was also effective in German Catholicism of the interwar period and increased the distance to the Weimar Republic. Also see Weiß, *Rechtskatholizismus*.
3   On this cf.: Loretan/Bernet-Strahm, *Das Kreuz der Kirche*; Brocker/Stein, *Christentum und Demokratie*; Isensee, *Keine Freiheit für den Irrtum*.
4   On this cf. the *Themenheft Concilium* 25 (1989) 1 '1789: Französische Revolution und Kirche'.
5   Such as, for instance, Austria's 'Christliche Ständestaat', cf.: Tálos/Neugebauer, *Austrofaschismus*.
6   Cf.: Scoppola, *La Proposta politica di De Gaspari*. I am grateful to Dr. Otto Weiß for this reference.
7   Such as, for instance, in the liturgical and the Catholic youth movements, although there were also crossovers, cf. for instance Klönne, 'Liturgische Bewegung'.
8   Tönnies, *Gemeinschaft und Gesellschaft*.
9   Evidence for the determinedly pro-democratic stance of the Catholic student body, for example, that was the consequence of the war experience, can already be found shortly after the war: Schmidtmann, *Katholische Studierende*. Also see: Damberg, 'Krieg, Theologie und Kriegserfahrung'. Damberg diagnoses that 'already during the Second World War [. . .] an increasingly dramatic dissonance developed [. . .] between the basic stock of religious interpretations of war ever since antiquity on the one hand [. . .] and the perceptions and questions of those who were directly affected on the other hand. Questions and stock answers match up less and less and the consequences of this are sure to extend far beyond the year 1945 and also far beyond the narrow field of debate regarding the always already existential phenomenon of war. It can be assumed that epochal changes of Church history and the theology of history were looming here'(214f.). According to this absolutely plausible conjecture the Second Vatican Council is part of the ecclesiastic process of coming to terms with its history during the totalitarian first half of the twentieth century and hence also with World War II.

10 Dubach, 'Communio-Ekklesiologie', 60.

11 Lehmann, 'Einleitung', 7.

12 On this cf. Bucher, 'Communio'.

13 Which can, however, develop very distinct forms, cf. Schivelbusch, *Kultur der Niederlage*.

14 Cf.: Hitler, *Mein Kampf*: 'Emperor William II was the first German Emperor to offer the hand of friendship to the Marxist leaders, not suspecting that they were scoundrels without any sense of honour. While they held the imperial hand in theirs, the other hand was already feeling for the dagger. There is no such thing as coming to an understanding with the Jews. It must be hard-and-fast 'Either-Or'. For my part I then decided that I would take up political work' (225).

15 Cf.: Niethammer, *Kollektive Identität*.

16 Cf.: Bucher, 'Entmonopolisierung und Machtverlust'.

17 Cf.: Klinger, *Das absolute Geheimnis*.

Personal Epilogue

That the ground of civilization is thin beneath our feet and that it is not threatened from the margins of society but first and foremost from society's centre has preoccupied me since my youth; the more so as I realized early on that evidence of this threat lay to the left and to the right of my paths.

The route to my grammar school passed between the Villa Wahnfried and the last residence of Houston Stewart Chamberlain. Chamberlain was Wagner's son-in-law and author of *Foundations of the Nineteenth Century* [*Grundlagen des neunzehnten Jahrhunderts*] one of the core texts of racist anti-Semitism. Winifred Wagner, though, the lady of Wahnfried and nearly wife of Hitler, declared her sympathies for Hitler as late as 1975, as well as her willingness to still receive him today were it possible, in Syberberg's film *Winifred Wagner und die Geschichte des Hauses Wahnfried 1914–1975*.

The route to my primary school, however, had passed by the Bayreuth synagogue that had remained standing because it was immediately adjacent to the Margravial Opera House which was not to be endangered. And it passed by the former 'House of German Education' – the seat of the nationwide 'National Socialist Teachers' Association'.

By and by I realized: 'The past is not dead; it is not even past. We cut ourselves off from it; we pretend to be strangers.'[1] (Christa Wolf). And then there was the tiny, dark coal cellar with the special door where – as our neighbour, who had become known to me lovingly as 'Auntie', told me – they had survived the bombings of Bayreuth in fear and anxiety.

The counter-world was the parish, the Catholic youth group which fostered my early appetite for discussion, my first infatuations and the thrilling new departures envisioned by the Second Vatican Council. The fact that on the trip to Poland in 1973 this counter-world did not evade the reality of Hitler and his victims was crucial. It led me to asking: What does the one have to do with the other? And: What was and is the response from my Catholic milieu to National Socialist Bayreuth?

Some answers have since proven disappointing: references to the (widespread) resistance from the Catholic milieu, or for example to the ecclesiastical hierarchy and its distance from Hitler. For the resistance of the milieu was also to a large part indifference toward the victims, the ecclesiastical hierarchy was – with a very few exceptions – itself politically and religiously blind towards Hitler.[2] It shocked me when I realized how naïve the faith of many – including many with responsibility – was back then when Hitler started getting a hold on Germany. The martyrs of Christian resistance, however – the Scholl siblings for instance, or Alfred Delp, Dietrich Bonhoeffer or Franz Jägerstätter, saints all of them, who we are duty bound to honour – they were rare, and who could presume to measure up against them, why, even just hope to be as clear-sighted and devout, steadfast and brave as they were?

How does faith help to avoid 'Brother Hitler's' seductions? Now, long before martyrdom?

We can recognize the temptations that are hidden within our own desires; we can identify human rights as God's political name and democracy as the method to protect them.[3] I discovered the third part of the answer earlier, before studying theology and also before academically engaging with Hitler, in a key scene for faith and also for liturgy: in the worship of the crucified Jesus.

The kind of theology we practice is not immaterial; it is not immaterial which God we believe in.

Notes

[1] Christa Wolf's novel *Patterns of Childhood* opens with this programmatic sentence.

[2] Cardinal Faulhaber's comment after a visit to Hitler on the Berghof in 1936 is quoted as one testimonial among many: 'The Reich Chancellor doubtlessly lives in faith with God. He acknowledges Christianity as the master-builder of western culture' (Volk, *Akten Kardinal Michael von Faulhabers II*, 194). Incidentally, nobody recognized this more clearly than the good and devout Catholic Adenauer. He wrote in 1946: 'I believe that had all the bishops on a given day opposed together from their pulpits, they could have averted much. This did not happen and there is no excuse for it. Had the bishops been imprisoned or deported to a concentration camp because of it, this would not have been a disgrace, on the contrary. None of this happened and so it is best to keep silent' (Denzler/Fabricius, *Die Kirche im Dritten Reich II*, 255).

[3] Cf.: Sander, *Macht in der Ohnmacht*. In relation to this question the Second Vatican Council still remains the basis all ecclesiastical existence today. For it is also a reckoning of the Church with its own anti-democratic past.

Glossary

Gau	geographical unit of territory designating a regional administrative district.
Gauleiter	head of one of the *Gaus*.
Gauparteitag	*Gau* Party Congress.
Gautag	District Day; official annual celebration.
Kampfzeit	'time of struggle'; The term refers to the early period of the Nazi Party, esp. in Munich, before it consolidated its power base.
Kreisleiter	district leader, party official subordinate to *Gauleiter*.
Lebensraum	living space; A key idea of National Socialist thought, this term connotes aggressive territorial expansion to create better living conditions for the German people.
Raum im Osten	'space in the East'; This connects with the ideas surrounding the *Lebensraum* as it was aimed specifically at expansion to the East.
Reichsbauernführer	Reich Farmers' Leader; official title of Richard Walther Dorré, who was Minister of Food and Agriculture from 1933.
'Reichsparteitag des Willens'	'Reich Political Party Rally of the Will'; the title given to the 1934 party rally to set it off from its annual counterparts.
Völkisch	nationalist; This was a late nineteenth- and early twentieth-century expression of German nationalism based on ethnicity.
Volksgemeinschaft	people's community; This was the key concept of the National Socialist ideology and described an ethnically and racially cleansed German nation based on a community held together by a sense of honour and spiritual mission.
Volksgenossen	members of the *Volksgemeinschaft*.

Volkskörper	the German people figured as a biological, racial unity.
Volkstum	the divinely created entity of German peoples. (This concept replaced nationality.)
Weihlied	an old German term for a song of consecration which is now closely associated with National Socialism where the term was used to connote religion in the context of secular; party political celebrations.
Winterhilfswerk	Winter Relief Programme; charitable programme aimed at providing the needy with food, clothing and fuel.

Bibliography

1. Unpublished sources

National Archives (Staatsarchiv), Nuremberg
NS Mischbestand (Sam. Streicher)
Municipal Archive (Stadtarchiv), Erlangen
Hitler-Reden: III.220.H.1.
Diocesan Archive (Diözesanarchiv), Rottenburg
Estate of Karl Adam (N 67):

Correspondence: Innerkirchliche Reform, Verhältnis Kirche-Reich (Nr. 31)
'Die geistige Lage des deutschen Katholizismus', Lecture in Aachen, 10 December
    1939 (Nr. 32)
'Deutsches Volkstum und katholisches Christentum' (Continuation) (Nr. 34)

2. Primary sources

Adam, K. (1933), 'Deutsches Volkstum und katholisches Christentum'. *Theologische Quartalschrift*, 114, 40–63.

—(1934a), 'Christus und das deutsche Volk'. *Deutsches Volksblatt*, 86 (18), 23 January.

—(1934b), 'Die Erlösungstat Jesu Christi'. *Deutsches Volksblatt*, 86 (19), 24 January.

—(1943/1944), 'Jesus, der Christus, und wir Deutsche'. *Wissenschaft und Weisheit*, 10 November, 73–103 and 10–23.

Berndt, A. -I. (1941), 'Vorwort', in H. Goedecke and W. Krug (eds), *Wir beginnen das Wunschkonzert für die Wehrmacht*. Berlin, pp. 7–8.

Brombacher, K. and E. Ritter, (eds) (1936), *Sendschreiben katholischer Deutscher an ihre Volks- und Glaubensgenossen* (2nd edn). Münster.

Domarus, M., (ed.) (2004), *Hitler: Speeches and Proclamations 1932–1945, 4 Volumes*. Wauconda, IL.

Faulhaber, M. (1933), *Das Alte Testament und seine Erfüllung im Christentum*. First Advent sermon by Cardinal Faulhaber in St. Michael on 3 December 1933. Munich.

Fröhlich, E., (ed.) (1987), *Die Tagebücher von Joseph Goebbels: Sämtliche Fragmente, Part 1: Aufzeichnungen 1923–1941, 4 Volumes*. Munich.

Genoud, F., (ed.) (1960), *The Testament of Adolf Hitler: The Hitler-Borman Documents, February–April 1945*. Translated by R. H. Stevens. London.

Hitler, A. (1939a), 'Der Führer vor dem ersten Reichstag Großdeutschlands'. Speech given at the Reichstag on 30 January 1939. Munich.

—(1939b), *Mein Kampf.* Translated from German by J. Murphy. London.

—(1942), *The Speeches of Adolf Hitler: April 1922–August 1939,* 2 Volumes. Translated from German by N. Baynes. London.

—(1980), *Sämtliche Aufzeichnungen 1905–1924,* E. Jäckel and A. Kuhn (eds). Stuttgart.

—(1988), *Monologe im Führerhauptquartier 1941–1944: Die Aufzeichnungen Heinrich Heims,* W. Jochmann (ed.). Bindlach.

—(1992ff.), *Reden, Schriften und Anordnungen Februar 1925–Januar 1933.* Munich. Volume 1: Die Wiedergründung der NSDAP: Februar 1925–Juni 1926 (1992); Volume 2: Vom Weimarer Parteitag bis zur Reichstagswahl: Juli 1926–Mai 1928 (2 Parts) (1992); Volume 3: Zwischen den Reichstagswahlen: Juli 1928–September 1930 (3 Parts) (1994f.); Volume 4: Von der Reichstagswahl bis zur Reichspräsidentenwahl: Oktober 1930–März 1932 (3 Parts) (1994 ff.); Volume 5: Von der Reichspräsidentenwahl bis zur Machtergreifung: April 1932–Januar 1933 (2 Parts), (1996/1998); Volume 6: Register, Karten und Nachträge, (2003).

Dokumentation Obersalzberg. Tondokumente: Täter, Gegner, Opfer (2003). [CD] Munich: Institut für Zeitgeschichte. (Edited by A. Feiber and V. Dahm.)

Lortz, J. (1926), *Katholische Renaissance oder dogmenfreie Religiosität? Ein Stück moderner Studentenseelsorge.* Würzburg.

—(1933), *Katholischer Zugang zum Nationalsozialismus.* Münster.

—(1934a), 'Katholisch und doch nationalsozialistisch'. *Germania,* 28 January.

—(1934b), 'Katholischer Zugang zum Nationalsozialismus: Ideologie oder Wirklichkeit?'. *Germania,* 4 February.

—(1934c), 'Unser Kampf um das Reich'. *Germania,* 6 May.

—(1935), 'Nationalsozialismus und Kirche', in J. Lortz, *Geschichte der Kirche in ideengeschichtlicher Betrachtung: Eine Sinndeutung der christlichen Vergangenheit in Grundzügen* (5th edn). Münster.

Phelps, R. (1968), 'Hitlers "grundlegende" Rede über den Antisemitismus'. *Vierteljahrshefte für Zeitgeschichte,* 16, 390–418.

Picker, H., (ed.) (1965), *Hitlers Tischgespräche im Führerhauptquartier 1941–1942* (new edn ed. P. Schramm). Stuttgart.

Schmaus, M. (1934), *Begegnungen zwischen katholischem Christentum und nationalsozialistischer Weltanschauung* (3rd edn). Münster.

Schmitt, C. (1934), 'Der Führer schützt das Recht: Zur Reichstagsrede Adolf Hitlers vom 13.7.1934'. *Deutsche Juristen-Zeitung,* 39, 945–50.

Simon, P. (1934), *Mythos oder Religion* (2nd edn). Paderborn.

Speer, A. (1970), *Inside the Third Reich.* Translated from German by R. and C. Winston. London.

Stasiewski, B., (ed.) (1968), *Akten deutscher Bischöfe über die Lage der Kirche 1933–1945, Volumem 1: 1933–1934.* Mainz.

Trevor-Roper, H. and François-Poncet, A., (eds) (1981), *Hitlers politisches Testament.* Hamburg.

Volk, L., (ed.) (1975/1978), *Akten Kardinal Michael von Faulhabers 1917–1945, Volume 1: 1917–1934, Volume 2: 1934–1945.* Mainz.

3. Secondary sources

1789: Französische Revolution und Kirche. (1981) Special Issue. *Concilium*, 25 (1).

Ackermann, J. (1970), *Himmler als Ideologe.* Göttingen.

Aly, G. (2005), *Hitlers Volksstaat: Raub, Rassenkrieg und nationaler Sozialismus.* Frankfurt/M.

Arnold, C. (2007), *Kleine Geschichte des Modernismus.* Freiburg.

Barkhaus, A. (1993), *Rasse: Zur Konstruktion des Begriffs im anthropologischen Diskurs der Aufklärung.* Ph. D. Universität Konstanz.

Bärsch, C. -E. (1987), *Erlösung und Vernichtung: Dr. phil. Goebbels – Zur Psyche und Ideologie eines jungen Nationalsozialisten.* Munich.

—(1989), 'Das Erhabene und der Nationalsozialismus'. *Merkur*, 43, 777–90.

—(2002), *Die Politische Religion des Nationalsozialismus* (2nd revised edn). Munich.

Bäumer, F. -J. (1996), ' " . . . weil Gesundheit, Rasse und Blut den 'Affekt des Herzens' Zeit besitzen" (L. Bopp, 1937): Zur katholischen Pastoraltheologie im Nationalsozialismus'. *Kirche und Judentum*, 11, 62–73.

—(2001), ' "O, Maria kennt die Werte, die in den Worten liegen: Blut und Boden": Zur katholischen Marienfrömmigkeit im Nationalsozialismus', in J. Heil and R. Kampling (eds), *Maria – Tochter Sion? Mariologie, Marienfrömmigkeit und Judenfeindschaft.* Paderborn, pp. 241–59.

Baumgartner, A. (1977), *Sehnsucht nach Gemeinschaft: Ideen und Strömungen im Katholizismus der Weimarer Republik.* Paderborn.

Baumgärtner, R. (1977), *Weltanschauungskampf im Dritten Reich: Die Auseinandersetzungen der Kirchen mit Alfred Rosenberg.* Mainz.

Bayer, O. and Peters, A. (1998), 'Art. Theologie', in J. Ritter and K. Gründer (eds), *Historisches Wörterbuch der Philosophie, Volume 10.* Basle, col. pp. 1080–95.

Becker, H. (1982), ' "Liturgie" im Dienst der Macht: Nationalsozialistischer Totenkult als säkularisierte christliche Paschafeier', in *Universität im Rathaus, Volume 2.* Mainz, pp. 56–86.

Behrenbeck, S. (1996), *Der Kult um die toten Helden: Nationalsozialistische Mythen, Riten und Symbole 1923–1945.* Vierow/Greifswald.

Bendel, R., (ed.) (2002), *Die Katholische Schuld? Katholizismus im Dritten Reich zwischen Arrangement und Widerstand.* Münster.

Berner, K. (2004), *Theorie des Bösen: Zur Hermeneutik destruktiver Verfügungen.* Neukirchen-Vluyn.

Bernhardt, R. (1999), *Was heißt 'Handeln Gottes'? Eine Rekonstruktion der Lehre von der Vorsehung.* Gütersloh.

Blaschke, O. (1997), *Katholizismus und Antisemitismus im Deutschen Kaiserreich.* Göttingen.

Bleistein, R. (1995), 'Abt Alban Schachleiter OSB: Zwischen Kirchentreue und Hitlerkult'. *Historisches Jahrbuch*, 115, 179–87.

Bollmus, R. (1970), *Das Amt Rosenberg und seine Gegner: Studien zum Machtkampf im nationalsozialistischen Herrschaftssystem.* Stuttgart.

Breuer, S. (1993), *Anatomie der Konservativen Revolution*. Darmstadt.

Breuning, K. (1969), *Die Vision des Reiches: Deutscher Katholizismus zwischen Demokratie und Diktatur, 1923–1934*. Munich.

Brocker, M. and Stein, T., (ed.) (2006), *Christentum und Demokratie*. Darmstadt.

Bröckling, U. (1993), *Katholische Intellektuelle in der Weimarer Republik: Zeitkritik bei Walter Dirks, Romano Guardini, Carl Schmitt, Ernst Michel und Heinrich Mertens*. Munich.

Broszat, M., Fröhlich, E. and Wiesemann, F., (eds) (1977), *Bayern in der NS-Zeit, Volume 1: Soziale Lage und politisches Verhalten im Spiegel vertraulicher Berichte*. Munich.

Bründl, J. (2002), *Masken des Bösen: Eine Theologie des Teufels*. Würzburg.

Bucher, R. (1998), *Kirchenbildung in der Moderne: Eine Untersuchung der Konstitutionsprinzipien der deutschen katholischen Kirche im 20. Jahrhundert*. Stuttgart.

—(2005), 'Entmonopolisierung und Machtverlust: Wie kam die Kirche in die Krise'? in R. Bucher (ed.), *Die Provokation der Krise* (2nd edn). Würzburg, pp. 11–29.

—(2006), 'Communio: Zur Kritik einer pastoralen Projektionsformel', in U. Feeser-Lichterfeld and R. Feiter (eds), *Dem Glauben Gestalt geben*. Münster, pp. 121–34.

Bucher, R., (ed.) (2005), *Die Provokation der Krise* (2nd edn). Würzburg.

Bücker, V. (1989), *Die Schulddiskussion im deutschen Katholizismus nach 1945*. Bochum.

Burkard, D. (2005), *Häresie und Mythus des 20. Jahrhunderts: Rosenbergs nationalsozialistische Weltanschauung vor dem Tribunal der römischen Inquisition*. Paderborn.

—(2007), 'Alois Hudal – ein Anti-Pacelli? Zur Diskussion um die Haltung des Vatikans gegenüber dem Nationalsozialismus'. *Zeitschrift für Religions- und Geistesgeschichte*, 59, 61–89.

Burkard, D. and Weiß, W., (eds) (2007), *Katholische Theologie im Nationalsozialismus, Volume 1: Institutionen und Strukturen*. Würzburg.

Burke, K. (1973), 'The Rhetoric of Hitler's "Battle"'. Reprinted in *The Philosophy of Literary Form: Studies in Symbolic Action* (3rd edn). Berkeley, pp. 191–220.

Cancik, H. (1980), '"Wir sind jetzt eins": Rhetorik und Mystik in einer Rede Hitlers (Nürnberg 11.9.1936)', in G. Kehrer (ed.), *Zur Religionsgeschichte der Bundesrepublik Deutschland*. Munich, pp. 13–48.

—(1982), '"Neuheiden" und totaler Staat: Völkische Religion am Ende der Weimarer Republik', in H. Cancik (ed.), *Religions- und Geistesgeschichte der Weimarer Republik*. Düsseldorf, pp. 176–212.

Cancik, H., (ed.) (1982), *Religions- und Geistesgeschichte der Weimarer Republik*. Düsseldorf.

Claret, B. (1997), *Geheimnis des Bösen: Zur Diskussion um den Teufel*. Innsbruck.

Claret, B., (ed.) (2007), *Theodizee: Das Böse in der Welt*. Darmstadt.

Cohn, N. (1961), *Das Ringen um das Tausendjährige Reich: Revolutionärer Messianismus im Mittelalter und sein Fortleben in den modernen totalitären Bewegungen*. Berne.

Conway, J. (1968), *The Nazi Persecution of Churches 1933–1945*. London.

Conzemius, V. (1990), 'Joseph Lortz – ein Kirchenhistoriker als Brückenbauer: Vom leichtfertigen Umgang mit Ideengeschichte und theologischer Geschichtsdeutung'. *Geschichte und Gegenwart*, 9, 247–78.

Dalferth, I. (2007), *Das Böse: Essay über die kulturelle Denkform des Unbegreiflichen.* Tübingen.

Damberg, W. (1993), 'Kirchengeschichte zwischen Demokratie und Diktatur: Georg Scheiber und Joseph Lortz in Münster 1933–1950', in L. Siegele-Wenschkewitz and C. Nicolaisen (eds), *Theologische Fakultäten im Nationalsozialismus.* Göttingen, pp. 145–67.

—(2007), 'Krieg, Theologie und Kriegserfahrung', in K. -J. Hummels and C. Kösters (eds), *Kirchen im Krieg: Europa 1939–1945.* Paderborn, pp. 203–15.

Danz, C. (2007), *Wirken Gottes: Zur Geschichte eines theologischen Grundbegriffs.* Neukirchen-Vluyn.

Denzler, G. (2003), *Widerstand ist nicht das richtige Wort: Katholische Priester, Bischöfe und Theologen im Dritten Reich.* Zurich.

Denzler, G. and Fabricius, V., (eds) (1984), *Die Kirche im Dritten Reich: Christen und Nazis Hand in Hand? Volume 2: Dokumente.* Frankfurt/M.

Diner, D. (1988), *Zivilisationsbruch: Denken nach Auschwitz.* Frankfurt/M.

Dröge, F. and Müller, M. (1995), *Die Macht der Schönheit: Avantgarde und Faschismus oder die Geburt der Massenkultur.* Hamburg.

Dubach, A. (1999), 'Die Communio-Ekklesiologie – eine zeitadäquate Konzeption von Kirche?', in B. Hilberath (ed.), *Communio – Ideal oder Zerrbild von Kommunikation?* Freiburg, pp. 54–68.

Dyck, J. (1997), *Rhetorik im Nationalsozialismus.* Tübingen.

Essner, C. (2002), *Die 'Nürnberger Gesetze' oder Die Verwaltung des Rassenwahns 1933–1945.* Paderborn.

Faber, R. and Gajek, E., (eds) (1997), *Politische Weihnacht in Antike und Moderne: Zur ideologischen Durchdringung des Fests der Feste.* Würzburg.

Falter, J. (1991), *Hitlers Wähler.* Darmstadt.

Fest, J. (1974), *Hitler.* Translated from German by R. Winston and C. Winston London.

Flasche, R. (1993), 'Vom Deutschen Kaiserreich zum Dritten Reich: Nationalreligiöse Bewegungen in der ersten Hälfte des 20. Jahrhunderts in Deutschland'. *Zeitschrift für Religionswissenschaft*, 1, 28–49.

Frei, N., (ed.) (2004), *Hitlers Eliten nach 1945* (2nd edn). Frankfurt/M.

Friedländer, S. (2006), *Das Dritte Reich und die Juden, Volume 2: Die Jahre der Vernichtung.* Munich.

—(2007), *Das Dritte Reich und die Juden, Volume 1: Die Jahre der Verfolgung* (3rd edn). Munich.

Fuchs, O. (2004), *Vom Segen des Krieges: Katholische Gebildete im Ersten Weltkrieg, Eine Studie zu Kriegsdeutung im akademischen Katholizismus.* Stuttgart.

—(2007), *Das Jüngste Gericht: Hoffnung und Gerechtigkeit.* Regensburg.

Gabriel, K. (1992), *Christentum zwischen Tradition und Postmoderne.* Freiburg.

Gabriel, K., (ed.) (1996), *Religiöse Individualisierung oder Säkularisierung? Biographie und Gruppe als Bezugspunkte moderner Religiosität.* Gütersloh.

Gajek, E. (2001), ' "Hohe Nacht der klaren Sterne" und andere "Stille Nacht" der Nationalsozialisten', in R. Faber (ed.), *Säkularisierung und Resakralisierung: Zur Geschichte des Kirchenliedes und seiner Rezeption.* Würzburg, pp. 145–64.

Gamm, H.-J. (1962), *Der braune Kult: Das Dritte Reich und seine Ersatzreligion.* Hamburg.

Gauchet, M. (1985), *Le désenchantement du monde: Une historique politique de la religion.* Paris.

Goodrick-Clarke, N. (2004), *The Occult Roots of Nazism: Secret Aryan Cults and their Influence on Nazi Ideology* (revised edn). London.

Gössmann, E. (2004), 'Katholische Theologie unter der Anklage des Nationalsozialismus: Zum zehnten Todestag von Michael Schmaus – aus Anlass einer jüngeren Veröffentlichung'. *Münchner Theologische Zeitschrift,* 55, 151–64.

Gotto, K. and Repgen, K., (eds) (1990), *Die Katholiken und das Dritte Reich* (3rd revised edn). Mainz.

Graml, H. (1993), 'Rassismus und Lebensraum: Völkermord im Zweiten Weltkrieg', in K. Bracher, M. Funke and H. Jacobson (eds), *Deutschland 1933–1945: Neue Studien zur nationalsozialistischen Herrschaft.* Düsseldorf, pp. 440–51.

Gregor, B. (1999), 'Zum protestantischen Antisemitismus: Evangelische Kirchen und Theologen in der Zeit des Nationalsozialismus', in Fritz Bauer Institut (ed.), *'Beseitigung des jüdischen Einflusses': Antisemitische Forschung, Eliten und Karrieren im Nationalsozialismus.* Frankfurt, pp. 171–200.

Greive, H. (1969), *Theologie und Ideologie: Katholizismus und Judentum in Deutschland und Österreich 1918–1935.* Heidelberg.

Grieswelle, D. (1972), *Propaganda der Friedlosigkeit: Eine Studie zu Hitlers Rhetorik 1920–1933.* Stuttgart.

—(1978), *Rhetorik und Politik: Kulturwissenschaftliche Studien.* Munich.

Gruber, H. (2006), *Katholische Kirche und Nationalsozialismus 1930–1945: Ein Bericht in Quellen.* Paderborn.

Grüttner, M. (1995), *Studenten im Dritten Reich.* Paderborn.

Gugenberger, E. (2001), *Hitlers Visionäre: Die okkulten Wegbereiter der Dritten Reiches.* Vienna.

Guillou, L. (1987), 'Die philosophische Gegenrevolution in Frankreich: L. de Bonald (1754–1840), J. de Maistre (1753–1821) und F. -R. de Chateaubriand (1768–1848)', in E. Coreth, W. Neidl and G. Pfligersdorfer (eds), *Christliche Philosophie im katholischen Denken des 19. und 20. Jahrhunderts,* Volume 1. Graz, pp. 445–58.

Haffner, S. (1978), *Anmerkungen zu Hitler,* Munich.

Hamann, B. (1999), *Hitler's Vienna: A Dictator's Apprenticeship.* Translated from German by T. Thornton. Oxford.

Hannot, W. (1990), *Die Judenfrage in der katholischen Tagespresse Deutschlands und Österreichs 1923–1933.* Mainz.

Heer, F. (1967), *Gottes erste Liebe: 2000 Jahre Judentum und Christentum – Genesis des österreichischen Katholiken Adolf Hitler.* Munich.

—(1968), *Der Glaube des Adolf Hitler.* Munich.

Heiber, H. (1991), *Universität unterm Hakenkreuz, Part 1: Der Professor im Dritten Reich: Bilder aus der akademischen Provinz.* Munich.

—(1992), *Universität unterm Hakenkreuz, Part 2: Die Kapitulation der Hohen Schulen, Volume 1.* Munich.

—(1994), *Universität unterm Hakenkreuz, Part 2: Die Kapitulation der Hohen Schulen, Volume 2.* Munich.

Heinsohn, G. (1995), *Warum Auschwitz? Hitlers Plan und die Ratlosigkeit der Nachwelt.* Reinbek.

Heinzmann, R. (1987), 'Die Identität des Christentums im Umbruch des 20. Jahrhunderts'. *Münchner Theologische Zeitschrift*, 38, 115–33.

Heitzer, H. (1993), 'Deutscher Katholizismus und "Bolschewismusgefahr" bis 1933'. *Historisches Jahrbuch*, 113, 354–87.

Heschel, S. (1999), 'Deutsche Theologen für Hitler: Walter Grundmann und das Eisenacher "Institut zur Erforschung und Beseitigung des jüdischen Einflusses auf das deutsche kirchliche Leben"', in Fritz Bauer Institut (ed.), *'Beseitigung des jüdischen Einflusses': Antisemitische Forschung, Eliten und Karrieren im Nationalsozialismus*. Frankfurt, pp. 147–67.

Hesemann, M. (2004), *Hitlers Religion: Die fatale Heilslehre des Nationalsozialismus*. Munich.

Hieronimus, E. (1982), 'Zur Religiosität der völkischen Bewegung', in H. Cancik (ed.), *Religions- und Geistesgeschichte der Weimarer Republik*. Düsseldorf, pp. 159–75.

—(1985), 'Zur Frage nach dem Politischen bei völkisch-religiösen Gruppierungen', in J. Taubes (ed.), *Der Fürst dieser Welt* (2nd edn). Munich, pp. 316–21.

Hödl, K., (ed.) (2005), *Der 'virtuelle Jude': Konstruktionen des Jüdischen*. Innsbruck.

Hoffmann, L. (1991), 'Das "Volk": Zur ideologischen Struktur eines unvermeidbaren Begriffs'. *Zeitschrift für Soziologie*, 20, 191–208.

Höhn, H. -J. (2003), *Versprechen: Das fragwürdige Ende der Zeit*. Würzburg.

Horst, U. (1992), 'Michael Schmaus: Glückwunsch zum 95. Geburtstag'. *Münchner Theologische Zeitschrift*, 43, 389–90.

Horstmann, J. and Liedhegener, A., (eds) (2001), *Konfession, Milieu, Moderne: Konzeptionelle Positionen und Kontroversen zur Geschichte von Katholizismus und Kirche im 19. und 20. Jahrhundert*. Schwerte.

Hoser, P. (1994), 'Hitler und die katholische Kirche: Zwei Briefe aus dem Jahre 1927'. *Vierteljahrshefte für Zeitgeschichte*, 42, 473–92.

Hummel, K. -J. (2004), *Zeitgeschichtliche Katholizismusforschung: Tatsachen, Deutungen, Fragen – Eine Zwischenbilanz*. Paderborn.

Hürten, H. (1992), *Deutsche Katholiken 1918–1945*. Paderborn.

Hüttenberger, P. (1977), 'Vorüberlegungen zum Widerstandsbegriff', in J. Kocka (ed.), *Theorien in der Praxis des Historikers*. Göttingen, pp. 117–34.

Iber, H. (1987), *Christlicher Glaube oder rassischer Mythus: Die Auseinandersetzung der Bekennenden Kirche mit Alfred Rosenbergs 'Der Mythus des 20. Jahrhunderts'*. Frankfurt/M.

Isensee, J. (1987), 'Keine Freiheit für den Irrtum: Die Kritik der katholischen Kirche an den Menschenrechten als staatsphilosophisches Paradigma'. *Zeitschrift der Savigny-Stiftung für Rechtsgeschichte* (Kan.Abt.), 104, 296–336.

Iserloh, E. (1979), 'Innerkirchliche Bewegungen und ihre Spiritualität', in H. Jedin (ed.), *Handbuch der Kirchengeschichte, Volume 7*. Freiburg, pp. 301–37.

—(1989), 'Joseph Lortz: Leben und ökumenische Bedeutung', in R. Decot (ed.), *Zum Gedenken an Joseph Lortz (1887–1975)*. Wiesbaden, pp. 3–11.

Jäckel, E. (1981), *Hitlers Weltanschauung* (revised and expanded edn). Stuttgart.

Karow, Y. (1994), 'Konstruktion und Funktion nationalsozialistischer Mythenbildung'. *Zeitschrift für Religionswissenschaft*, 2, 145–60.

—(1997), *Deutsches Opfer: Kultische Selbstauslöschung auf den Reichsparteitagen der NSDAP*. Berlin.

Kater, M. (1975), *Studentenschaft und Rechtsradikalismus in Deutschland 1918–1933: Eine sozialgeschichtliche Studie zur Bildungskrise in der Weimarer Republik*. Hamburg.

Kershaw, I. (1987), *The Hitler Myth*. Oxford.

—(1998), *Hitler, Volume 1: Hubris 1889–1936*. London.

—(2000), *Hitler, Volume 2: Nemesis 1936–1945*. London.

Klinger, E. (1994), *Das absolute Geheimnis im Alltag entdecken: Zur spirituellen Theologie Karl Rahners*. Würzburg.

Klönne, A. (1991), 'Die Liturgische Bewegung – "erblich" belastet? Historisch-soziologische Fragestellungen zur Vorgeschichte der Liturgiekonstitution', in H. Becker, B. Hilberath and U. Willers (eds), *Gottesdienst, Kirche, Gesellschaft*. St. Ottilien, pp. 13–21.

Kluge, U. (2006), *Die Weimarer Republik*. Paderborn.

Knauft, W. (1998), *Konrad von Preysing – Anwalt des Rechts: Der erste Berliner Kardinal und seine Zeit*. Berlin.

Kocher, R. (1993), *Herausgeforderter Vorsehungsglaube: Die Lehre von der Vorsehung im Horizont der gegenwärtigen Theologie*. St. Ottilien.

Köhler, J. (2001), 'Adolf Kardinal Bertram (1859–1945): Sein Umgang mit dem totalitären System des Nationalsozialismus', in H. -J. Karp and Köhler, J. (eds), *Katholische Kirche unter nationalsozialistischer und kommunistischer Diktatur*. Cologne, pp. 175–93.

Kreidler, H. (1983), 'Karl Adam und der Nationalsozialismus', *Rottenburger Jahrbuch für Kirchengeschichte*, 2, 129–40.

—(1988), *Eine Theologie des Lebens: Grundzüge im theologischen Denken Karl Adams*. Mainz.

Kretschmar, G. (1971–2000), *Dokumente zur Kirchenpolitik des Dritten Reiches*, 4 Volumes. Munich.

Krieg, R. (1992), *Karl Adam: Catholicism in German Culture*. Notre Dame, Indiana.

Künneth, W. (1947), *Der große Abfall: Eine geschichtstheologische Untersuchung der Begegnung zwischen Nationalsozialismus und Christentum*. Hamburg.

Langer, M. (1995), *Alois Hudal, Bischof zwischen Kreuz und Hakenkreuz: Versuch einer Biographie*. Ph. D. Vienna.

Lautenschläger, G. (1987), *Joseph Lortz (1887–1975): Weg, Umwelt und Wert eines katholischen Kirchenhistorikers*. Würzburg.

—(1989), 'Neuere Forschungsergebnisse zum Thema: Joseph Lortz', in R. Decot (ed.), *Zum Gedenken an Joseph Lortz (1887–1975)*. Wiesbaden, pp. 293–313.

Lehmann, M. (2002), 'Einleitung', in M. Lehman (ed.), *Parochie: Chancen und Risiken der Orstgemeinde*. Leipzig, pp. 7–17.

Lepsius, O. (1994), *Die gegensatzaufhebende Begriffsbildung: Methodenentwicklungen in der Weimarer Republik und ihr Verhältnis zur Ideologisierung der Rechtswissenschaft im Nationalsozialismus*. Munich.

Leugers, A. (1989/1990), 'Adolf Kardinal Bertram als Vorsitzender der Bischofskonferenz während der Kriegsjahre (1939–1945)'. *Archiv für schlesische Kirchengeschichte*, 47, 7–35.

—(1996), *Gegen eine Mauer bischöflichen Schweigens: Der Ausschuss für Ordensangelegenheiten und seine Widerstandskonzeption*. Frankfurt/M.

—(2004), 'Positionen der Bischöfe zum Nationalsozialismus und zur national-sozialistischen Staatsautorität', in R. Bendel (ed.), *Die katholische Schuld?*

Katholizismus im Dritten Reich – Zwischen Arrangement und Widerstand (2nd revised edn). Münster, pp. 122–42.

Ley, M. (1993), *Genozid und Heilserwartung: Zum nationalsozialistischen Mord am europäischen Judentum*. Vienna.

Ley, M. and Schoeps, J., (eds) (1997), *Der Nationalsozialismus als politische Religion*. Bodenheim.

Liebmann, M. (1988), 'Bischof Hudal und der Nationalsozialismus: Rom und die Steiermark'. *Geschichte und Gegenwart*, 7, 263–80.

Lindgens, G. (1985), *Freiheit, Demokratie und pluralistische Gesellschaft in der Sicht der katholischen Kirche: Dokumente*. Stuttgart.

Loretan, A. and Bernet-Strahm, T., (eds) (2006), *Das Kreuz der Kirche mit der Demokratie: Zum Verhältnis von katholischer Kirche und Rechtsstaat*. Zurich.

Lukacs, J. (1997), *The Hitler of History*. London.

Lutz, H. (1970), *Katholizismus und Faschismus: Analyse einer Nachbarschaft. H. Lutz antwortet C. Amery*. Düsseldorf.

Maier, H. (2004), *Das Doppelgesicht des Religiösen: Religion, Gewalt, Politik*. Freiburg.

Maier, H., (ed.) (1996), *'Totalitarismus' und 'politische Religionen': Konzepte des Diktaturvergleichs*. Paderborn.

Maistre, J. (2007), *Vom Papst: Ausgewählte Texte*. Berlin.

Manemann, J. (2002), *Carl Schmitt und die politische Theologie*. Münster.

Mann, T. (1939), 'That Man is my Brother'. *Esquire*, 11 (3), 3 March, 31, 132.

Marcowitz, R. (2007), *Die Weimarer Republik 1929–1933* (2nd edn). Darmstadt.

Maurer, R. (1985), 'Chiliasmus und Gesellschaftsreligion: Thesen zur politischen Theologie', in J. Taubes (ed.), *Der Fürst dieser Welt* (2nd edn). Munich, pp. 117–35.

Meier, H. (1994), *Die Lehre Carl Schmitts: Vier Kapitel zur Unterscheidung Politischer Theologie und Politischer Philosophie*. Stuttgart.

Meier, K. (1996), *Die Theologischen Fakultäten im Dritten Reich*. Berlin.

Mendlewitsch, D. (1988), *Volk und Heil: Vordenker des Nationalsozialismus im 19. Jahrhundert*. Rheda-Wiedenbrück.

Menozzi, D. (1989), 'Bedeutung der katholischen Reaktion auf die Revolution'. *Concilium*, 25, 51–8.

Miles, R. (2003), *Racism* (2nd edn). London.

Morsey, R., (ed.) (1988), *Katholizismus, Verfassungsstaat und Demokratie: Vom Vormärz bis 1933*. Paderborn.

Naumann, M. (1984), *Strukturwandel des Heroismus: Vom sakralen zum revolutionären Heldentum*. Königstein.

Niethammer, L. (2000), *Kollektive Identität: Heimliche Quellen einer unheimlichen Konjunktur*. Reinbek.

Ogan, B. and Weiss, W., (eds) (1992), *Faszination und Gewalt: Zur politischen Ästhetik des Nationalsozialismus*. Nuremberg.

Peukert, D. (1982), *Volksgenossen und Gemeinschaftsfremde: Anpassung, Ausmerze und Aufbegehren unter dem Nationalsozialismus*. Cologne.

—(1989), *Max Webers Diagnose der Moderne*. Göttingen.

Poliakov, L. (1993), *Der arische Mythos: Zu den Quellen von Rassismus und Nationalismus*. Hamburg.

Prieberg, F. (2000), *Musik im NS-Staat*. Cologne.

Reck, N. (2001), 'Der Gott der Täter: Subjektverbergung, Objektivismus und Un-/Schulddiskurse in der Theologie', in K. v. Kellenbach, B. Krondorfer and N. Reck (eds), *Von Gott reden im Land der Täter.* Darmstadt, pp. 29–45.

—(2005), '"Wer nicht dabeigewesen ist, kann es nicht beurteilen": Diskurse über Nationalsozialismus, Holocaust und Schuld in der Perspektive verschiedener Generationen'. *Münchner Theologische Zeitschrift,* 56, 342–54.

—(2006), '" . . . er verfolgt die Schuld der Väter an den Söhnen und Enkeln, an der dritten und vierten Generation" (Ex 34,7): Nationalsozialismus, Holocaust und Schuld in den Augen dreier katholischer Generationen', in B. Krondorfer, K. v. Kellenbach and N. Reck (eds), *Mit Blick auf die Täter: Fragen an die deutsche Theologie nach 1945.* Gütersloh, pp. 171–252.

Reichel, P. (1991), *Der schöne Schein des Dritten Reiches: Faszination und Gewalt des Faschismus.* Munich.

Reichelt, W. (1991), *Das Braune Evangelium: Hitler und die NS-Liturgie.* Wuppertal.

Reifferscheid, G. (1975), *Das Bistum Ermland und das Dritte Reich.* Cologne.

Repgen, K. (1978), 'Über die Entstehung der Reichkonkordats-Offerte im Frühjahr 1933 und die Bedeutung des Reichskonkordats: Kritische Bemerkung zu einem neuen Buch'. *Vierteljahrshefte für Zeitgeschichte,* 26, 499–534.

—(1987), 'Reichskonkordats-Kontroversen und historische Logik', in M. Funke, H. Jacobsen, H. -H. Knütter and H. -P. Schwarz (eds), *Demokratie und Diktatur: Geist und Gestalt politischer Herrschaft in Deutschland und Europa* (FS K. -D. Bracher). Bonn, pp. 158–77.

Rhodes, J. (1980), *The Hitler Movement: A Modern Millenarian Movement.* Stanford.

Rissmann, M. (2001), *Hitlers Gott: Vorsehungsglaube und Sendungsbewusstsein des deutschen Diktators.* Zurich.

Rödel, U., Frankenberg, G. and Dubiel, H., (eds) (1989), *Die demokratische Frage.* Frankfurt/M.

Rösch, A. (1985), *Kampf gegen den Nationalsozialismus.* Frankfurt/M.

Ruster, T. (1994), *Die verlorene Nützlichkeit der Religion: Katholizismus und Moderne in der Weimarer Republik.* Paderborn.

Rüthers, B. (1988), *Entartetes Recht: Rechtlehren und Kronjuristen im Dritten Reich.* Munich.

Safranski, R. (1997), *Das Böse: Oder das Drama der Freiheit.* Munich.

Sander, H. -J. (1999), *Macht in der Ohnmacht: Eine Theologie der Menschenrechte.* Freiburg.

Scheel, K. (1996), *Der Tag von Potsdam.* Berlin.

Scheliha, A. (1999), *Der Glaube an die göttliche Vorsehung: Eine religionssoziologische, geschichtsphilosophische und theologiegeschichtliche Untersuchung.* Stuttgart.

Scherzberg, L. (2001), *Kirchenreform mit Hilfe des Nationalsozialismus: Karl Adam als kontextueller Theologe.* Darmstadt.

—(2005), 'Das kirchenreformerische Programm pro-nationalsozialistischer Theologen' in L. Scherzberg (ed.), *Theologie und Vergangenheitsbewältigung.* Paderborn, pp. 56–70.

Schirrmacher, T. (2007), *Hitlers Kriegsreligion.* Bonn.

Schivelbusch, W. (2001), *Die Kultur der Niederlage.* Berlin.

Schmidbaur, H. (2004), *Gottes Handeln in Welt und Geschichte: Eine trinitarische Theologie der Vorsehung.* St. Ottilien.

Schmidt-Biggemann, W. (2004), *Politische Theologen der Gegenaufklärung*. Berlin.

Schmidtmann, C. (2006), *Katholische Studierende 1945–1973: Eine Studie zur Kultur- und Sozialgeschichte der Bundesrepublik Deutschland*. Paderborn.

Schmölders, C. (1997), 'Die Stimme des Bösen: Zur Klanggestalt des Dritten Reiches'. *Merkur*, 51, 681–93.

Schneider, T. and Ullrich, L., (eds) (1988), *Vorsehung und Handeln Gottes*. Leipzig.

Schnurbein, S. and Ulbricht, J., (eds) (2001), *Völkische Religion und Krisen der Moderne: Entwürfe 'arteigener' Glaubenssysteme seit der Jahrhundertwende*. Würzburg.

Scholder, K. (1977), *Die Kirchen und das Dritte Reich, Volume 1: Vorgeschichte und Zeit der Illusionen*. Frankfurt/M.

—(1978), 'Altes und Neues zur Vorgeschichte des Reichskonkordats: Eine Erwiderung auf Konrad Repgens'. *Vierteljahrshefte für Zeitgeschichte*, 26, 535–70.

—(1985), *Die Kirchen und das Dritte Reich, Volume 2: Das Jahr der Ernüchterung 1934: Barmen und Rom*. Frankfurt/M.

Scholl , I. (1993), *Die Weiße Rose* (revised edn). Frankfurt/M.

Schrage, W. (2005), *Die Vorsehung Gottes? Zur Rede von der providentia Dei in der Antike und im Neuen Testament*. Neukirchen-Vluyn.

Schreiber, G. (1988), *Hitler – Interpretationen 1923–1983: Ergebnisse, Methoden und Probleme der Forschung* (2nd revised edn). Darmstadt.

Schulze, H. (1982), *Weimar: Deutschland 1917–1933*. Berlin.

Schuster, P. -K. (1998), *Nationalsozialismus und 'Entartete Kunst'* (5th revised edn). Munich.

Schwan, A. (1980), 'Zeitgenössische Philosophie und Theologie in ihrem Verhältnis zur Weimarer Republik', in K. Erdmann and H. Schulze (eds), Weimar: *Selbstpreisgabe einer Demokratie*. Düsseldorf, pp. 259–85.

Scoppola, P. (1977), *La Proposta politica di De Gaspari*. Bologna.

Siebenrock, R. (2005) 'Theologischer Kommentar zur Erklärung über die religiöse Freiheit Dignitatis humanae', in P. Hünemann and B. Hilberath (eds), *Herders Theologischer Kommentar zum Zweiten Vatikanischen Konzil, Volume 4*. Freiburg, pp. 125–218.

Sieferle, R. (1992), 'Die Konservative Revolution und das "Dritte Reich"', in D. Harth and J. Assmann (eds), *Revolution und Mythos*. Frankfurt/M, pp. 178–205.

Siegele-Wenschkewitz, L. (1974), *Nationalsozialismus und Kirche: Religionspolitik von Partei und Staat bis 1935*. Düsseldorf.

Siegele-Wenschkewitz, L., (ed.) (1994), *Christlicher Antijudaismus und Antisemitismus: Theologische und kirchliche Programme deutscher Christen*. Frankfurt/M.

Siegele-Wenschkewitz, L. and Nicolaisen, C., (eds) (1993), *Theologische Fakultäten im Natinalsozialismus*. Göttingen.

Smelser, R. (1989), *Robert Ley, Hitlers Mann an der 'Arbeitsfront': Eine Biographie*. Paderborn.

Sofsky, W. (1996), *Traktat über die Gewalt*. Frankfurt/M.

Sonne, H. (1975), *Die Politische Theologie der Deutschen Christen*. Göttingen.

Sontheimer, K. (1978), *Antidemokratisches Denken in der Weimarer Republik: Die politischen Ideen des deutschen Nationalismus zwischen 1918 und 1933*. Munich.

Soosten, J. (1993), 'Civil Society: Zum Auftakt der neueren demokratietheoretischen Debatte mit Seitenblick auf Religion, Kirch und Öffentlichkeit'. *Zeitschrift für evangelische Ethik*, 37, 139–57.

Spicer, K. (2002), 'Gespaltene Loyalität: "Braune Priester" im Dritten Reich am Beispiel der Diözese Berlin'. *Historisches Jahrbuch*, 122, 287–320.

Stangl, B. (1985), *Untersuchungen zur Diskussion um die Demokratie im deutschen Katholizismus unter besonderer Berücksichtigung ihrer Grundlagen und Beurteilung in den päpstlichen Stellungnahmen und konziliaren Entscheidungen.* Munich.

Tallgren, V. (1981), *Hitler und die Helden: Heroismus und Weltanschauung.* Helsinki.

Tálos, E. and Neugebauer, W., (eds) (2005), *Austrofaschismus* (5th edn). Münster.

Tönnies, F. (1988 [1887]), *Gemeinschaft und Gesellschaft: Grundbegriffe der reinen Soziologie.* Darmstadt.

Tooze, J. (2007), *Ökonomie der Zerstörung: Die Geschichte der Wirtschaft im Nationalsozialismus.* Munich.

Tyrell, A. (1975), *Vom 'Trommler' zum 'Führer': Der Wandel von Hitlers Selbstverständnis zwischen 1919 und 1924 und die Entwicklung der NSDAP.* Munich.

Valverde, C. (1987), 'Juan Donoso Cordés (1809–1853)', in E. Coreth, W. Neidl and G. Pfligersdorfer (eds), *Christliche Philosophie im katholischen Denken des 19. und 20. Jahrhundert, Volume 1: Neue Ansätze im 19. Jahrhundert.* Graz, pp. 649–66.

Voegelin, E. (1986 [1938]), *Political Religions.* Translated from German by T. J. DiNapoli and E. S. Easterly III. Lewiston, NY.

Vogt, M. (1997), *Sozialdarwinismus: Wissenschaftstheorie, politische und theologisch-ethische Aspekte der Evolutionstheorie.* Freiburg.

Volk, L. (1972), *Das Reichskonkordat vom 20. Juli 1933.* Mainz.

—(1987), *Katholische Kirche und Nationalsozialismus: Ausgewählte Aufsätze.* Mainz.

Vondung, K. (1971), *Magie und Manipulation: Ideologischer Kult und politische Religion des Nationalsozialismus.* Göttingen.

—(1988), *Apokalypse in Deutschland.* Munich.

Wacker, B., (ed.) (1994), *Die eigentlich katholische Verschärfung: Konfession, Theologie und Politik im Werk Carl Schmitts.* Munich.

Walkenhorst, P. (1996), 'Nationalismus als "politische Religion"? Zur religiösen Dimension nationalistischer Ideologie im Kaiserreich', in O. Blaschke and F. -M. Kuhlemann (eds), *Religion im Kaiserreich: Milieus, Mentalitäten, Krisen.* Gütersloh, pp. 503–29.

Wegener, F. (2004), *Heinrich Himmler: Deutscher Spiritismus, französischer Okkultismus und der Reichsführer SS.* Gladbeck.

Weingart, P., Kroll, J. and Bayertz, K. (1988), *Rasse, Blut und Gene: Geschichte der Eugenik und Rassenhygiene in Deutschland.* Frankfurt/M.

Weiss, O. (1995), *Der Modernismus in Deutschland: Ein Beitrag zur Theologiegeschichte.* Regensburg.

Whitehead, A. (1926), *Religion in the Making.* Cambridge.

Willnauer, E. (2005), *Heute das Böse denken: Mit Immanuel Kant und Hannah Arendt zu einem Neuansatz für die Theologie.* Berlin.

Winkler, H. (1993), *'Weimar 1918–1933': Die Geschichte der ersten deutschen Demokratie.* Munich.

Wippermann, W. (1989), *Der konsequente Wahn: Ideologie und Politik Adolf Hitlers.* Munich.

Wippermann, W., (ed.) (1986), *Kontroversen um Hitler.* Frankfurt/M.

Wittstadt, K. (1982), 'Die Katholisch-theologische Fakultät der Universität Würzburg während der Zeit des Dritten Rieches', in P. Baumgart (ed.), *Vierhundert Jahre Universität Würzburg.* Neustadt/Aisch, pp. 399–429.

Wolf, C. (1980), *Patterns of Childhood* [formerly *A Model Childhood*]. Translated from German by U. Molinaro and H. Rappolt. New York.

Wolf, H., (ed.) (1998), *Antimodernismus und Modernismus in der katholischen Kirche: Beiträge zum theologiegeschichtlichen Vorfeld des II. Vatikanums.* Paderborn.

Wolf, H. and Arnold, C., (eds) (2001), *Der Rheinische Reformkreis: Dokumente zu Modernismus und Reformkatholizismus 1942–1955, 2 Volumes.* Paderborn.

Wulf, C. and Kamper, D., (eds) (1987), *Das Heilige: Seine Spur in der Moderne.* Frankfurt/M.

Zitelmann, R. (1999), *Hitler: The Policies of Seduction.* Translated from German by H. Bogler. London.

Index